Intimacy
Human and Divine

Sandra Holt is a former computer-programmer and lecturer living in rural Aberdeenshire where her husband is minister to a Church of Scotland congregation. An experienced spiritual director, Sandra divides her time between writing, guiding people through the Spiritual Exercises of Ignatius of Loyola, facilitating retreats, and being taxi-driver for her three busy children. *Intimacy Human and Divine* is her first book.

For my husband Jack
and children
Jonathan, Adam and Sarah

Intimacy
Human and Divine

Sandra Holt

Published in Great Britain in 2001 by
Society for Promoting Christian Knowledge
Holy Trinity Church
Marylebone Road
London NW1 4DU

Biblical quotations are, unless otherwise stated, from
The Jerusalem Bible © 1966 by Darton, Longman & Todd Ltd
and Doubleday and Co. Inc.

British Library Cataloguing-in-Publication Data

A catalogue record for this book is available
from the British Library

ISBN 0–281–05388–X

Typeset by Pioneer Associates, Perthshire
Printed in Great Britain by
Omnia Books, Glasgow

Contents

Introduction   1

1   You Have Ravished My Heart   14

2   Encountering God Beneath the Sheets   31

3   Come and See   49

4   They Have Run Out of Wine   63

5   Do You Know What I Have Done to You?   77

6   Unless You Become Like Little Children   94

7   What Do You Want?   110

8   But If It Dies . . .   125

9   Do You Love Me?   143

Introduction

Better to marry than be aflame with passion.

So advised Paul in his first letter to the church folk at Corinth. His concern was a pastoral one entirely specific to the first-century Church. Since Paul expected the imminent return of Jesus and the establishing of a new order he thought it sensible for those not already committed to spouse and family to remain single and free to devote themselves to the worship and service of God for the brief time left. But only if passions could be controlled.

I am reminded of the joke concerning a Roman Catholic priest and a churchman from the Scottish highlands. Both are attending a wedding reception and stand chatting politely together. A waiter approaches and proffers a tray of well-filled whisky glasses. The priest accepts a glass but his companion is affronted. 'I would rather commit adultery than put that glass to my lips!' he exclaims. With alacrity the priest returns his glass to the tray saying merrily: 'I didn't realize there was a choice.' Paul put before the Corinth folk a choice that seemed to fit the circumstances. Unfortunately many Christians still think they must choose between passionate union with someone they love and a relationship of depth with God. Nothing could be further from the truth.

It is natural to long for human intimacy, to wish to know and be fully known by someone we love. Many of us also long for a more intimate relationship with God. This book will help us pursue both. It is a book for those who, like Paul (perhaps even because of Paul), have not made the connection between humanity's longing for intimacy and God's desire for an intimate encounter with us – those who fear that since human intimacy includes sex it must somehow exclude God. But better to marry than be aflame with passion. Why not both? There is no need to choose between love of partner and love of God, between intimacy with partner and intimacy with God. Desire for passionate intimacy with a loving partner is my sexuality and this has a spiritual connection that can lead me to a deeper intimacy with God. Conversely, desire for intimacy with God is my spirituality and this has a sexual connection that can lead me to a new depth of passionate intimacy with my partner. Both my sexuality and my spirituality, intimacy human and divine, are gifts from God. There is no need to choose between our partner and God. We can be passionately intimate with both.

This book pursues intimacy human and divine and trusts that from them will proceed a deeper intimacy with family, community, humanity and all of creation. It trusts too that those living the celibate life and those couples living in a committed relationship but without undertaking marriage vows will find much that is said connecting with their own desires for intimacy human and divine. An exploration of the subject of intimacy cannot help but connect us with the joy and sorrow of others: one other, a few others, all others, and even with the suffering and joy of the incarnate Son.

There can be little doubt that we all need to make these connections if we are to discover the life God has in mind for humanity. Ironically it has never been easier to talk, email, fax or for that matter to fly round the globe for face-to-face meetings with friends, family, colleagues, customers. Walk down any main street and you will encounter all sorts of people making connections on mobile phones: chatting, laughing, changing plans. Communication has never been so affordable or easy. But still intimacy seems to elude us and few are enjoying a burning passion about life.

John's Gospel tells us that we love because God loved us first. I think the same is true of intimacy. We long for it because God passionately longed for intimacy with us first. God is the author of passionate communion and its most determined advocate. God is the one who burns with longing. Intimacy with and for creation is God's choice and only intention. It is *the* promise sown into our very being. I believe the vague or restless desire many of us feel for something beyond our present experience of life, love, faith and passion is our awareness of this promise.

With this awareness as a starting point this book explores the following:

⅄ Passionate intimacy both with God and with our partner is our destiny but it is also an invitation
⅄ While we long for intimacy we also resist it
⅄ The quest for intimacy is a prayer quest but it involves risk and requires disclosure

Intimacy Human and Divine

⋏ Intimacy is a playful celebration of life yet takes us to
the heart of the Christian faith: the passion of Christ.

Our explorations into these paradoxes will not be exhaus-
tive and I trust will raise more questions for reflection,
further reading and discussion than have yet occurred to
me. That being said, let me set out the premise of this
particular book and its approach.

The premise is simple: intimacy is a grace. Grace is
the sufficiency of God ceaselessly creating and recreating
what is good and it is also individual gifts from that sufficiency. No amount of human knowledge or work or
wanting will produce grace in us. That is why this book
differs from all others you may have read on the subject
of personal relationships. It is not a self-help or self-
development manual. It assumes that self cannot develop
independently of God's sufficiency. As Paul observed: 'In
him we live and move and exist' (Acts 17.28).

It was Albert Einstein who pondered that there are only
two ways of approaching life: either nothing in it is a
miracle or everything is. This book declares the same
about grace. All life is gift. Marriage is a grace, the mobile
phone is a grace, one truly intimate encounter between
two people is a grace. All the good we see is grace.

Imagine a young person born with the gift of music.
To liberate her own musical genius she will seek out a
master musician, become the pupil, and enter a disciplined
and often rigorous programme of training that demands
her all but feels like life. Not all of us are musical geniuses
but we are all born with the gift of intimacy. The only
master of the intimacy genius is God, so our quest for life
must lead us not into a regime or programme but into

4

prayer. In prayer we ask for the grace of intimacy to be liberated within us. This is not, however, the kind of asking that holds out an empty hand and expects to have it filled. I am not the helpless infant of an omnipotent if kindly patriarch. I am the gifted disciple of a wise and passionate maestro who desires that my inherent genius grow strong and confident.

So when I pray for the grace of intimacy I expect to be shown where to go, what to do, who to attend to, in order to co-operate with the God of all grace. There is nothing passive here. My whole personality and psychology, my energy, enthusiasms, desires, fears, inclinations and disinclinations: all of these form the locus of my prayer. I take responsibility for all of it while seeking in it all God's loving intention for me, for the world, for the whole of creation. When I ask for the grace of intimacy I acknowledge that fearfully and wonderfully made I may be, but nevertheless God is the sufficiency of my life. All is grace.

As Mother Julian of Norwich discovered:

> I am the ground of your praying. First, it is my will that you have something, and then I make you want it too; then I make you beseech me for it – and you do beseech me. So how could you not have what you ask for?

> (*Revelations of Divine Love*)

Intimacy is the grace God had in mind for us since before time began. Intimacy is our genius and the answer to all our questions about the purpose of life. Our pursuit of intimacy with partner and/or with God is as significant in God's loving plan for creation as the incarnation of the Son.

Now since intimacy is a grace it follows that no matter how assiduously you read this book, how many of the suggested exercises you try, how much you want and will to go deeper into intimacy nothing will change, except by the grace of God 'whose power, working in us, can do infinitely more than we can ask or imagine . . .' (Ephesians 3.20).

What of those who believe that nothing in life is a miracle of grace? I believe that the plethora of self-development books lining the walls of our major bookstores testifies to the reality of a longing for *something more* felt by us all. Many people who will not take God into consideration eagerly abandon themselves into the hands of these authors in the hope that what worked for one can work for all. But what worked for them was grace, even if they did not recognize it as such, and only grace will transform our situation. And grace cannot be captured in a formula or process. Grace is free and will not be summoned from the pages of a book. Grace is something we can only invite and grace comes to each person in a uniquely personal way. Those who will not ask God's help either pace among the bookshelves seeking a do-it-yourself miracle cure for their hunger or they seek to quiet their longing with numerous distractions and with lives dedicated to lesser gods.

All grace comes from God, in God's time and in God's measure. I write this book because I am confident that intimacy is a grace God gives freely, generously and joyfully even before we ask for it. However it lies within our choice as free beings to co-operate with God's loving intention by being attentive to the grace. One way of being attentive is by bringing ourselves and our experience of life to God in a prayer that is both incarnational and contemplative. James Nelson (1992) describes the incarnational approach:

> It does not begin with broad doctrinal formulations about God and humanity. Rather, it begins with the bodily experiences of life: making breakfast and making love; beef burgundy and bloated bellies of starving children; daily calendars and deadly carcinomas; missives we pen to those we love and missiles we aim at those we fear. It begins with the many big and little birthings we encounter daily.

For over 500 years people wishing to make themselves and their bodily experience of life available to God have found the spirituality of Ignatius of Loyola extremely helpful. Best known as the founder of the Jesuit religious order, Ignatius was a romantic man and lived in sixteenth-century Spain in a romantic age of knights and liege lords. He dreamed of deeds of great valour before his soldiering days came to an abrupt and violent end. While convalescing from a near-fatal wound Ignatius fell in love with Christ and dreamed again of deeds of heroic service for his Lord.

The years that followed this conversion, years of following Christ as faithful companion, convinced Ignatius that each of us can have intimate experience of God in our ordinary lives and most importantly that each of us can make sense of what we experience. From his own experience and that of guiding others Ignatius wrote a small book entitled *The Spiritual Exercises*. These exercises are the basis for a prayer retreat that has become increasingly popular since its rediscovery and reformation by the Jesuits in 1965. It is primarily a retreat aimed at those who have a strong desire for a deeper, more intimate relationship with God.

From his own experience Ignatius said: 'There are very few who realize what God would make of them if they abandoned themselves entirely into his hands, and let themselves be formed by his will.' His is a spirituality of 'the more'. Not 'more' in any acquisitive sense, rather it is the more of deep and unreserved abandonment to intimacy that is possible between two persons, or between a person and God.

The approach this book takes to the pursuit of intimacy is a contemplative and incarnational one arising out of my own interest in Ignatian thought and practice. Ignatius was a day-dreamer by nature so it was almost by accident that he discovered that day-dreaming about, or contemplating, the life of Christ was a qualitatively different experience from any other of his day-dreams.

'The Word of God is something alive and active' (Hebrews 4.12) – so Scripture says of itself. The Scripture is God-breathed and is still breathing. When this alive and active Word speaks to us about Jesus we find ourselves encountering the living Lord. Though he lived two thousand years ago we are still able to develop an intimate relationship together.

In this book we will seek to co-operate with God's desire of intimacy with and for us by turning to Scripture and disposing ourselves to an intimate relationship with Jesus by contemplating his life and reflecting on our own. Relying on the promises of the Master – 'To have seen me is to have seen the Father' (John 14.9) and 'The Father and I are one' (John 10.30) – we will abandon ourselves into God's hands and discover what God would make of us, our relationships, our faith.

If contemplative prayer is new to you do not worry. Contemplation is not difficult. To contemplate is simply to gaze at something with leisure, as we do in a day-dream. We are all contemplatives to some degree. We have all stood and gazed at a beautiful vista or at a sleeping child. We know that when we take time to gaze with leisure at beauty our hearts feel the benefit. Or when we gaze and really notice the television pictures of starving children in another country, we are affected by what we are seeing and hearing. Often it is the little details easily missed with a more hurried glance that move us most. Perhaps a fly that sits on an infant's eyelid because the child has no energy even to swat it away.

If I gaze long enough, the scene before me has a chance to do even more than motivate me to donate some time or money for famine relief. The encounter with this child or that vista can address me and my life. This is contemplation. And while I can contemplate a vista I encounter on a walk, say, I can also contemplate the memory of that encounter. This is what William Wordsworth refers to in his poem 'The Daffodils':

> For oft, when on my couch I lie, in vacant or in
>   pensive mood,
> They flash upon the inward eye, which is the bliss
>   of solitude.
> And then my heart with pleasure fills, and dances
>   with the daffodils.

Wordsworth knew that he had not exhausted the good-ness of that daffodil host simply because he eventually turned from it to retrace his steps home. The inward eye he speaks of is our facility for imaginative contemplation.

None of us ever plumb the depths of meaning offered by any experience, in one go. If I walk along a lakeside, and come upon a host of daffodils dancing in the breeze my heart soars. I feel better, more alive for the encounter. I sense gratitude. This encounter holds more for me than all of these. More joy, more life, more gratitude, possibly even more truth about the meaning and direction of my life, than I perceive immediately. Well might I take some solitary time to allow this body of flowers to flash upon my inward eye, to surprise me again, to fill me with yet more pleasure, and to give me their message of hope. Again and again, I might find fruit in the repetition of this encounter, in my imagination.

This is not new to any of us. We testify to the truth of it each time we watch a video of a family celebration, a wedding or a holiday. There are things we had not noticed at the time: a child sucking his thumb behind the bride, a grandparent dozing in a chair. We can see, enjoy, celebrate, understand more each time we look at the video.

A contemplative attitude to Scripture and to life helps us to co-operate with God's call to intimacy. Contemplation of a personal relationship is another. Casting an honest gaze on this allows God a say, a chance to shape for us and with us a new and deeper intimacy. You can explore your own facility for contemplation by relaxing for ten minutes or so and gazing contemplatively at this book in the light of your experience of it thus far. Give yourself some time and a quiet space for this – the experience should be a relaxed and leisurely one.

▲ Close the book and hold it in your hand. Look at the book.

▲ Take your time and notice the dimensions of it, the colours and texture and weight . . . notice the illustration and the title . . . ponder these . . .

▲ What pleases you about this physical book?

▲ Does anything jar with you about it?

▲ Read the title out loud once or twice and observe how you feel . . . (try reading it in different ways: proclaiming the title, whispering it, etc.).

▲ Recall noticing this book for the first time in the bookshop or library or on your friend's coffee table . . . replay that scene like a video in your imagination . . . let it pass before your inward eye . . . notice your mood at the time . . . your physical condition . . . the last thought you can recall just before encountering the book.

▲ What was it that prompted you to pick it up?

▲ What were you hoping the book would offer?

▲ And when you read the back cover or skimmed the introduction – what if anything attracted you, or disturbed you, or made your heart beat a little faster?

▲ And now, at this moment – what is it you desire for your relationship with your partner?

▲ What do you desire for your relationship with God?

Let your responses bubble up inside you. Try to avoid too much thinking. This is an exercise in leisurely gazing and noticing. It does not require too much thought. You will find it useful to note down any responses, but don't be side-tracked into evaluation of them. Imagine that each response is a messenger arriving at your door after a long journey through difficult terrain. Try to open the door wide and welcomingly. Usher the messenger in and listen carefully to the message borne all this way for your sake. Be generous with your ear and slow with your judgements. It is enough for now to receive the message accurately. There will be time later to search out its meaning and significance.

⋏ Once all the responses have 'arrived' and are noted down, read them over.
⋏ Highlight any that feel particularly important or moving or surprising or uncomfortable.

Perhaps an example will help. I ponder the question: What prompted me to pick this book up and bring it home? My response might be:

⋏ an attractive spine caught my eye;
⋏ when I turned it over the picture and colour pleased me;
⋏ when I read the title I was intrigued. It didn't give much away, but neither did it impose too much;
⋏ the introduction made me hope this book would address my unspoken longing for more in the most personal areas of my life.

Any or all of these responses may 'arrive' and in any order. Further responses may arrive now or as I go about my daily business. One question can open the door to a host of messengers, arriving like magi from the far places of my own soul. All bearing gifts. And one question will lead to another and another... What is the *'more'* I am looking for beyond the visible experience of my life?

Now, in the light of this time of noticing your attractions and resistances to this book and its subject – how do you feel? What might you need from God to enable you to really pursue your desires?

Perhaps already you can identify a need for radical honesty when reflecting on the material of this book and its effect on you. You want to be as open and honest with yourself as possible on the quest for intimacy but sense this could be difficult. Even honesty is a grace. Whatever your felt need God is the sufficiency of your life. You can, for example, ask for the grace of an honesty more radical than you, on your own, feel capable of. God who loves and desires you will take seriously your prayer for the graces only God can give. This intimate God might well reply to the prayer for radical honesty thus: 'Do not be afraid, for I have redeemed you, I have called you by your name. You are mine' (Isaiah 43.1). With this assurance, we are ready to begin.

References

Mother Julian of Norwich, *Revelations of Divine Love*. London, Hodder & Stoughton Christian Classics, 1987.

Munitiz, Joseph A. and Endean, Philip (translated and notes by), *Saint Ignatius of Loyola, Personal Writings*. London, Penguin, 1996.

Nelson, James, *The Intimate Connection*. London, SPCK, 1992.

Wordsworth, William, 'The Daffodils', in Francis Turner Palgrave (ed.), *Palgrave's Golden Treasury*. Oxford, Oxford University Press, 1994.

1

You Have Ravished My Heart

Intimacy is our destiny.

This is what poets, artists, composers, novelists, film-makers try to convey with words and pictures and music. Often they focus on the 'love at first sight' phenomenon rather than the more usual experience of a gradual increase in the intensity of our feelings for another.

Still, any of us who have loved will no doubt be able to remember glimpsing the subject of our love from across a room or coming down the street and feeling our heart lurch in recognition and anticipation of an encounter. Whether or not it is love at first sight or love at the two thousandth sight matters not. This jolting encounter with our destined other is a most fruitful place to begin our contemplative prayer for the grace of intimacy. Spend some time with the memory of it. Recall the variety of sensations: touch, sounds, sights, tastes, fragrances that were a part of it. Try to remember and gaze in leisure at that moment when you realized: this other is meant for me.

Here is how one lover described it:

You have ravished my heart, my sister bride.

14

You have ravished my heart with one of your eyes,
With one gem from your necklace.

(Song of Songs 4.9)

You have ravished my heart. Is that how it felt for you?
As though the doors to your heart had been broken off
their hinges by one glance from that other and could
never again be closed to him or her? I hope so. I hope we
have all known this feeling. I hope we still do.

These passionate declarations are part of 'The Song of
Songs' – the most unusual piece of literature to be included
in the Old Testament. It is a graphic and erotic account of
the burning desires and passionate appetites aroused by
love; a poem that luxuriously paints a picture of the
encounter, the courtship, the passion, the pains and the
endurance of love. In it a young couple flout the strictures
of convention to meet secretly and explore their new
love with kisses, caresses, and finally with a longed-for
consummation. The Song contains many passages that
can be very fruitfully contemplated by any of us yearning
either to return and refresh our first love or desiring a yet
deeper intimacy in our relationship.

We might begin by reflecting on those lines:

You have ravished my heart with one of your eyes,
With one gem from your necklace.

In your imagination look into the eyes of your partner.
What is it you see there that is attractive? What promise
is there, what comfort, what mystery? If the eyes are the
window of a person's soul then what is it about this
person's soul that can ravish your own? Your partner may
not wear a necklace but he or she will have some gems of

his/her own. What is the one gem that never fails in its allurement, moving you to admiration, surprise, desire?

The Song also describes our subsequent day-dreams about the person with whom we have so dramatically fallen in love:

> The sound of my beloved.
> Behold, he comes,
> Leaping over the mountains,
> Springing over the hills,
> Resembling, my beloved, a gazelle
> Or a young stag, the hart.
>
> (Song of Songs 2.8, 9)

Become alert to your own day-dreams and responses to the anticipated return of your partner after a time of parting. Similarly become aware of yourself returning from work, play, etc. In what, if any, ways do you feel yourself leaping over mountains and springing over hills in your impatience to meet up again? Imagine your partner as an animal. Which one? Perhaps different animals at different times or in different moods: the gazelle is fast, the young stag is too but it also speaks, to me at least, of vulnerability. What animal is your partner and which one might you be?

Love never runs smoothly and in the Song we read of the torments the young lovers endure at times of parting and of misunderstanding:

> I nearly died,
> My mind went blank,
> My heavy heart with sickness sank
> In awful black dejection.

Into the city streets I ran,
Searching here, calling there.

(Song of Songs 5.6)

I am sure we all recognize that sick feeling and black dejection. What is the worst thing about the inevitable tensions and conflicts of your relationship? What happens to you physically, emotionally, mentally when things go wrong? The woman in the Song ran into the streets searching for her lover. What is your reaction to an argument or to a betrayal real or imagined? What helps the situation? What hinders reconciliation but gives you some satisfaction at the time?

In spite of all the difficulties, the lovers in the Song joyfully anticipate and directly invite sexual union:

Spread me among the raisin cakes,
Lay me out among the apples,
For faint with love am I.

(Song of Songs 2.5)

This passage, with its reference to the little raisin cakes used in fertility festivals, is best contemplated while soaking in a warm bath filled with fragrant bubbles or oils and surrounded by candles with soft music playing and a glass of wine to hand. It is such a sensual passage that it almost demands a sensual approach to its contemplation. So relax and allow yourself the luxury of becoming aware of your own unique sensuality. Imagine the last time you were panting with desire, when you were faint with love or in passionate pursuit. Whether or not you said and did the things that desire suggested to you, imagine yourself saying and doing them now. Fantasize a little and set free the poet-lover within you.

Consummated love is a delight that the Song proclaims in poetry:

I have entered my garden, my sister bride.
I have gathered my myrrh, together with my spice.
I have eaten my honeycomb, together with my honey.
I have drunk my wine, along with my milk.

(Song of Songs 5.1)

What does consummation mean for you? When you make love what is it that is being consummated? And is it fragrant like myrrh, delicious like honey, celebratory like wine? Does your relationship still have its own secret garden, known only by you two?

Amid the passion and eroticism the Song declares the eternal strength and primacy of love:

Place me as a seal upon your heart,
As a signet upon your arm.
For strong as death is love.
Jealous as Sheol, relentless.
Her darts, darts of fire, a flame of Yah.
Many waters are not able to quench love
And torrents shall not sweep it away.

(Song of Songs 8.6, 7)

How would you express your own commitment to this intimate relationship? Perhaps rings were exchanged when you married, perhaps you exchange anniversary gifts each year, but consider ways in which you can place each other as a seal upon your hearts on a more frequent basis. Life is busy and we are too easily driven into each day's busyness without taking even two minutes to plot its direction. As a couple we need to insist on time to re-affirm together the direction in which we desire the relationship to move. Remember the wise advice 'never let the sun go down on your wrath'? Invaluable though it is, more is required for the modern relationship. We should make an effort never to let the sun rise on our relationship without a simple acknowledgement of its primacy not only in our lives but most particularly in the day ahead.

The three lines that follow the passage above contain a timely warning for us all:

> If a man should give
> All the wealth of his home, for love,
> They would utterly scorn him.
>
> (Song of Songs 8.7)

Wealth is not our destiny, intimacy is. Sadly we are all too easily made deaf to the primacy of love's call on us by the siren of the market. We act as though loving intimacy were just another possession that can be acquired, often at a bargain price, and then stored for future use. So a man cries in disbelief as his wife leaves him: 'But I gave her everything she wanted!' While a woman bitterly tells her friends: 'He took the best 30 years of my life, and now he's left me with nothing.' Love cannot be bought or bartered. It is above and beyond any commercial transaction.

Contemplating these passages from the Song can be done alone of course but they will yield yet more fruit if you try it with your willing partner:

- Gaze into each other's eyes and tell one another what you see there.
- Describe to one another how you feel when anticipating a reunion after a busy day at the office.

19

⌃ Write and exchange letters gently listing the effects of conflict on you and your hopes and ideas for a better way of handling these difficult times.

⌃ Share a bath or shower together and reminisce on past passionate unions while arousing desire for the next one.

⌃ Develop together a new vocabulary to describe the significance of consummation of your love and the experience of sexual climax and try it out. This can be as light-hearted an exercise as you care to make it, or as poetic.

⌃ Agree to give the relationship primacy in your life (as though deep intimacy were indeed your destiny) and consider together how that must affect the most ordinary things of daily life.

I realize the word 'primacy' when applied to any but the faith relationship may send shivers up the spines of some readers. Surely, I hear you say, my partner must come second to God in my affection and priorities? Well yes and no.

I would agree wholeheartedly that the first and principal relationship in the life of a Christian person is that to God in whom, after all, we live and move and have our very being. However I think it likely that, in a misguided effort to make this so, many of us have overlooked the rather obvious fact that God is inclined to view a couple as one. Indeed the New Testament suggests that God views whole families along with their household servants as one, and this inclusion may go even further.

There is a story told of the conversion to Christianity of a tribal chief. The missionaries tell the new convert to return in the morning for his baptism. Imagine their surprise when morning dawns and the chief along with his tribe turns up to be baptized. For the missionaries a personal decision for God is required by each one of these people, but as far as this tribal family is concerned it is one in, all in. I think God may very well see things the same way. None of us comes to God alone. We all come in community. One in, all in. The One of course being Jesus Christ.

So though we may feel uneasy about God coming second to our partner, God may be delighted with the situation. If truth were told, coming second like this would be, in many cases, promotion for God. I suspect that most of my fervent attempts to put God first have occurred at times when neither God nor partner has been anything like as important to me as my own self. And of course there is no fooling God about this.

Consider this common enough situation among sincere Christian people. The husband sits in church one morning and listens as a plea is made for people to help with the youth club on a Friday night. The man's heart is stirred and immediately after the service he goes forward to offer help. Then he goes home to his wife and four pre-school children. He tells her of his decision and as her face shows her disbelief he rushes to reassure her that this is as difficult for him as for her but it is clearly a call from God. The man is already committed to three evenings every week doing God's work in the parish. He often justifies his activities with the thought that God is coming first in his life. God, however, is bemused.

Giving primacy to our relationship with God is a tricky business. Men and women often get it wrong, confusing God's desire for the world with their own drives and

21

desires for security, success, recognition and other riches. Whenever the Church has zealously sought to put God first she has made her most disastrous mistakes: the Crusades, the Inquisition, the witch-hunts, and more recently rampant homophobia. The Church can still unintentionally direct people to put God first in their relationships by putting human love a very poor second. It will come as no surprise when the man so keen to sacrifice his family to become the saviour of the parish youth club turns out to be the parish priest.

When we dare as people of faith to give primacy to the relationship we are developing with our partner we are on slightly surer ground and almost inevitably are following the lead and will of God for us. After all, if we cannot love the brother (or sister) who is bodily present to us how can we ever hope to love God who is Spirit? God is not asking me to choose between body and spirit, God and my partner, but between Christ and the world. No matter how much energy and focus I give to this human relationship, God does not fear exclusion. This intimacy I am developing with my husband is an authentic and sacred path to intimacy with God. God not only knows this but has ordained it so.

That is why when we have contemplated the Song of Songs individually and with our partner we have still not exhausted its riches. For the Song of Songs is a God-breathed piece of literature that addresses not only the triumphs and trials, the thrills and spills, of human intimacy but also those involved in restless longing for intimacy with God. While it speaks of a human lover who ravishes my heart it also proclaims the presence of a Divine Lover who does the same.

John Donne encountered this Divine Lover and uses the most passionate and even violent language in his 'Holy Sonnets XIV' to capture something of the earth-shattering effect on him:

> Batter my heart, three person'd God; for you
> As yet but knocke, breathe, shine, and seeke to mend;
> That I may arise, and stand, o'erthrow mee, and bend
> Your force, to break, blowe, burn and make me new.
> I, like an usurpt towne, to'another due,
> Labour to'admit you, but Oh, to no end,
> Reason your viceroy in mee, mee should defend,
> But is captiv'd and proves weake or untrue.
> Yet dearely I love you, 'and would be loved faine,
> But am betroth'd unto your enemie;
> Divorce mee, untie, or break that knot againe,
> Take mee to you, imprison mee, for I
> Except you enthrall mee, never shall be free,
> Nor ever chaste, except you ravish me.

Try reading the whole sonnet out loud. Try to read it without emotion. 'For I except you enthrall mee, never shall be free, Nor ever chaste, except you ravish me.' Impossible isn't it? Every word proclaims the burning desire of the poet to surrender to Love and his anguish at finding himself unequal to the consummation that Love intends with him.

More than one commentator on the Song of Songs considers it a purely secular piece of literature since God is not mentioned in it at all. I think Ignatius would disagree. His experience of life and faith taught him that God could be found in all situations: in a prison as easily as in a church, in Paris as in Jerusalem, in poverty or sickness as well as in riches and health. God is there to be discovered in all of these and more. God can be found in the Gospels and in a piece of erotic poetry. Even in the absence of any mention of God the Song speaks passionately to the reader of this Divine Lover encountered by Donne. It tells the ancient story of the ecstatic torments that are part and parcel of such an encounter.

Like Donne, St John of the Cross also knew the ecstasy and torment of an encounter with the living God. His 'Spiritual Canticle' incorporates whole lines from the Song of Songs and is both a dramatic love poem and allegory of divine love. Of the reasons behind the 'Spiritual Canticle' he says:

> And who can set in words that which He makes them to feel? And lastly who can express that which He makes them desire? Of a surety, none; nay, indeed, not the very souls through whom He passes. It is for this reason that, by means of figures, comparisons and similitudes, they allow something of that which they feel to overflow and utter secret mysteries from the abundance of the Spirit, rather than explain these things rationally.

The Song expresses in words of poetry the secret mysteries about God's love and the possibilities of intimacy with the Divine Lover. Countless believers down through the ages have read the Song and discovered God's presence and their own destiny in the words and emotions. Perhaps you will too. You will certainly find it interesting, possibly surprising and I hope fruitful to repeat the contemplations of our seven passages from the Song of Songs at least once more. This time imagine, as St John of the Cross did, that

God is the lover and you the beloved. God says to you:

> You have ravished my heart, my sister bride.
> You have ravished my heart with one of your eyes,
>
> (Song of Songs 4.9)

Men will find it useful to note that the young girl whose words make up the greatest part of this dialogue is by no means a coy and passive beauty waiting for her prince to awaken her with a kiss. She is feisty and determined, pursuing love with tenacity and courage. She is a very modern woman in love with a modern man. Recall too that St John of the Cross often expressed himself in poetry as the beloved and God as the lover in pursuit, even speaking of himself as 'she' in 'O Living Flame of Love':

> O living flame of love,
> How tenderly you wound
> My soul in her profoundest core!
> Do it now I ask you:
> Break the membrane of our sweet union.

Both male and female can contemplate the Song and make use of its imagery to discover deeper truths within their own hearts and experience. Imagine, for example, that God is the one waiting in anticipation of an encounter with you and sees you as a gazelle, as a young stag leaping over the mountains. Consider too that God would just as easily and enthusiastically spring over the hills to come to you. Try to imagine the black dejection God experiences when something comes between you two. How God would run out into the street, risking any danger for just a glimpse of you and the chance to reconcile you to him/her.

Dare to take that sensual bath and as you soak, become aware with all of your senses of the God who is faint with love for you. And since the Song of Songs is about two lovers you might reflect on your own desire and passion for God and for consummation of that love in the mystical union of intimacy. Again St John of the Cross (in 'Dark Night') gives a new vocabulary for expressing this union with God. A vocabulary which would serve equally well to describe the moments of ecstasy we can enjoy with our partner:

> I lay. Forgot my being,
> And on my love I leaned my face.
> All ceased. I left my being,
> Leaving my cares to fade
> Among the lilies far away.

Can we imagine ourselves forgetting our being, our worries, everything but this loved other on whom we lay? Dare we imagine God experiencing this with us and we with God?

Before its inclusion in the Old Testament the Song was already known and extensively used as entertainment at celebrations and harvest festivals, weddings and reunions to express something of the mystery of intimacy, both human and divine. But most surprisingly it later became an important part of the liturgy at the annual feast of Passover when Israel remembered and gave thanks for her exodus from Egypt. The reason is simple. The Song of Songs communicates in a most effective way the intimacy that results from being whole and complete in relation to another. The Song is a contemplation of salvation, not only of a whole people, as in the story of

26

exodus, but of a few, even of a couple. Intimacy, the Song declares, *is* our salvation.

Isn't that exactly the experience we encounter when first we realize that this other is meant for us? It is a feeling of being saved, of finally being made whole, completed by an entwining of heart, mind, soul with this other.

Intimacy is salvation. It is exodus from the captivity of a meaningless existence, from the daily round of making bricks from not quite enough straw. It is liberation and a beckoning journey to the promised land in the lively, passionate, dynamic and erotic company of this person we love. This at least was the experience of Ignatius and one he was confident that those who made the 30-day retreat of the Spiritual Exercises could share.

Those involved in the counselling of couples observe that the person we fall in love with is our twin. Counsellors and psychologists explain this by pointing to our child-hood development. During childhood while some of our personality is allowed to develop, other bits are not. This is because none of us has a perfect childhood. We sustain hurts, need to defend ourselves from threats real or per-ceived and consequently bits of our self are shut down for the sake of survival. Now when our hormones set us off in search of a mate it is these hidden but powerful parts of ourselves that seek out the one person in this world who will redeem our damaged self. We look for a person who is still firing in the areas we have shut down. And when we are fortunate to encounter this other, it feels as though we have known him or her forever. We were meant for one another.

We are attracted to people because their visible quali-ties are qualities we also possess and which long to be set free and given full reign in our personalities.

Then perhaps we are attracted to Jesus because we recognize something in him that is part of us too. A part that was there at creation was shut down as the world developed and only waits to be re-awakened, redeemed by intimacy. After all, when God created heaven and earth and all of life God affirmed the inherent goodness of it all.

The Song of Songs declares that God is indeed our twin and union with God our destiny. It offers a passionate glimpse of our salvation and a graphic description of the difficulties to be overcome on our exodus to the promised land.

Anyone who is familiar with the Spiritual Exercises of Ignatius will realize that a person praying through them is also on an exodus journey and through contemplative prayer of the gospel meets in Jesus their twin. Recognizing in him all those areas of personal, devotional, and community life where the fires of love have been shut down is an encounter that leaves the senses reeling, the world turned upside down and a shout of wonder on the retreatant's lips. With a heart ravished by this revelation of love the praying person turns again to contemplate the gospel passages. He or she seeks the loved one in them, day-dreaming of his looks, words, actions, and most importantly becoming aware of his intention for a deepening intimacy with the one praying.

The experience is strikingly similar to the girl in the Song who is struck with love and then goes in pursuit of its fulfilment. She is conscious of her natural beauty but conscious too of her lowly status. She describes herself to her lover as a mere 'crocus of the Sharon, a lily of the valleys'. With her unsightly sunburnt skin she can hardly believe that she is looked upon with desire.

Do not look at me because I am black-black,
Because the sun has scorched me.

(Song of Songs 1.6)

But she surrenders graciously to the truth of love: that beauty is in the eyes of the beholder. Just as surely the praying person comes to acknowledge with gratitude and wonder and no small measure of relief that 'the man whom God loves has not any value in himself. His value consists simply in the fact that God loves him' (Buttrick, 1956).

The girl in the Song finds herself day-dreaming about her lover and with every encounter, real or imagined love and admiration grows. She longs not only for sexual union, the consummation of their growing love and devotion, but also for a time when their love could be openly seen by all:

O for the freedom of kinship familiar,
Then would I kiss you with open abandon,
With no disapproval from many cold stares.

(Song of Songs 8.1)

From within a strict cultural setting she speaks of a freedom only possible if her lover were instead her older brother. Then she could throw her arms around him in public without causing scandal. This sense of freedom that accompanies kinship familiar is an experience often reported by those who spend some time, as during the Spiritual Exercises, contemplating the life of Christ. People speak of a growing ease between themselves and Christ, more even than one might attribute to a developing friendship. It is as though the mind of Christ and the mind of the praying person are becoming akin.

Like the Spiritual Exercises the Song of Songs invites us to discover the possibilities for and the difficulties besetting intimacy with another and with The Other. We could usefully spend many hours contemplating its message, allowing its passion to address our own ardent desire (or lack of desire) for the intimacy God intends.

One man, defining his experience of erotic intimacy with his partner, tries to describe how they have shared deeply of their desires, fantasies, hopes and sensual delights. They have shown their love by deeds and words. With passion aflame they have worshipped the other with their unambiguous bodies. Each kiss a loving approach, each caress a tender exploration and invitation to surrender. Both feel like gods. Empowered, creative, loved into wholeness by this other. Redeemed by this twin. Set free from fear and isolation. Set free for life and love. He spoke of the post-coital recognition that 'I have been for her everything she wanted and she has been for me everything I wanted'. This depth of intimacy with none other than God is our destiny.

References

Buttrick, George A. (ed.), *The Interpreter's Bible*. New York, Abingdon Press, 1956.

Donne, John, 'Holy Sonnets XIV' in *The Oxford Anthology of English Verse*. Oxford, Oxford University Press, 1986.

Gledhill, Tom, *The Message of The Song of Songs*. Leicester, IVP, 1994.

St John of the Cross, 'Spiritual Canticle', 'O Living Flame of Love' and 'Dark Night', in Barnstone, Willis (ed.), *The Poems of St John of the Cross*. New York, New Directions Publishing Corporation, 1972.

2

Encountering God Beneath the Sheets

Intimacy is never the beginning.

First there is encounter. During the course of an ordinary day I encounter many people: family, friends, colleagues, clients, fellow commuters, tradesmen, officials, shop-keepers. Some are face-to-face encounters, some are over the phone or by email. They vary in duration, content, effect and significance. All of them have one thing at least in common: the potential for intimacy. An encounter becomes intimate when I share something of who I am and you reciprocate – when we step tentatively over the conventional civilities and on to the holy ground of rela-tionship and shared humanity. Through such encounters we begin to know and be known by ourselves, each other and by God. Each day the grace of intimacy is there for us in these ordinary encounters. But the choice is ours. Meeting a neighbour on the street we can go for the grace, or we can go for the bus. No encounter is necessarily intimate.

In a world where intimacy is not nurtured or encour-aged, where neighbours are strangers, shops are huge precincts of anonymity and the workplace a jungle, we consider ourselves fortunate to find one person with whom we can allow ourselves to be truly known. Statistics regarding marriage may lead us to doubt and even to despair but the fact remains that for many of us ordinary life includes commitment to an intimate relationship with a partner. And we expect that the relationship will endure, sense that it can become richer, deeper, *more*, with every experience shared and through each daily encounter of our two souls.

Ignatius would agree. He would expect the ordinary experience of this relationship to be holy ground for both souls. A place worth approaching with reverence and attention. An encounter that quietly insists we take off our sandals, stop rushing about, pause, observe, really take note. An intimate place of meaning and significance, full of spiritual depth and creative eros.

But even encounters with our partner can be superficial. Meeting round the breakfast table we can go for the grace or for the cereal packet. Often there is no time for anything deeper than pleasantries during a busy day until we fall at last, exhausted, into the bed we share together. Then it is indeed fortunate that beneath the sheets is an excellent place to encounter not only my partner but my God. A place to develop intimacy with both.

Does this notion make you uncomfortable? If so this could be because long ago the Church developed a dualistic view of life and love. The Church believed in the hierarchical division of the person into two parts: body and soul. True spirituality was a function of the soul. It was celibate and sprung from self-giving love. Sex was necessary for propagation but being of the body was deeply damaging to spiritual progress and in need of stringent control. In the Middle Ages the Church exercised control over the sex lives of ordinary people with rules regarding the days of the year when sexual activity was prohibited for the sake of the soul. These eventually numbered over 280, in addition to days when a woman was menstruating, pregnant or in the post-natal period!

Thankfully the Church's obsessive control lessened as time wore on but the influence of Luther, who considered sex to be unclean, and Calvin, who considered sexual pleasure to be somewhat evil because of its passion, ensured that the basic message remained unchanged: sexuality was the enemy of spirituality. Love of God and universal love of mankind were both sanctified but passionate, erotic love between two people was dangerous and defiling.

In ancient Greek there are actually four words for love: *agape* (self-giving), *eros* (desire for fulfilment), *epithymia* (libido) and *philia* (friendship). Each word is an attempt to capture one dimension of love, and as James Nelson (1992) points out:

> Each dimension needs the others for love's wholeness. Without eros, agape is cold and devoid of energizing passion. Without philia, epithymia becomes a sexual contract. Without epithymia, other ways of loving become bloodless. Without agape, the other dimensions of loving lose their self-giving, transformative power.

Nowadays the Church would agree but we would be naive to underestimate the influence her earlier bias still exerts. Society's plunge into ever more outrageous manifestations of libido divorced from *philia*, *agape* and true *eros* is surely just the latest rebellion against dualism. It is as poignant a reaction to the oppressive control of mother Church as the repressed sexuality of Victorian times ever was. And what about the *agape* love offered by the Church? Is it not growing cold and empty of energizing passion? Could this be the reason for dwindling church membership? Would *eros* not provide the missing fulfilment through intimate communion that would draw the people into the Church?

James L. Empereur SJ (1998) finds in his pastoral work as a priest that the dualistic view is still very much alive:

> A fragmenting dualism is especially obvious in the area of sexuality. That we find it unimaginable that sexual intercourse can be a form of prayer comes home to me each time during a marriage preparation session when I ask the couple if sexual union will be part of their prayer. Some few indicate that it will; others seem puzzled by the question; some react with fear and even a kind of horror. Despite all the efforts made by spiritual writers and practitioners as well as feminists to overcome this dualistic approach we still lack the kind of integration of matter and spirit required if spirituality and sexuality are to become partners in our movement toward God.

This dualistic view of life and faith has served us ill. Fortunately an alternative has always been present both in the Jewish religion and even in the Christian Church. The twelfth-century Yorkshire Cistercian, Aelred of Rievaulx believed that when two lovers have sex, Christ is present between them much as the Holy Spirit is understood to be present with the Father and the Son.

It might be worth pausing to reflect on Aelred's idea for a while. Begin by contemplating the picture you have of the Trinity. How do you understand the relation of the Holy Spirit to, and her presence with, the Father and the Son? Is it a committee meeting with the Holy Spirit busily fetching coffee and taking notes on a spiral pad as the Father and Son discuss the family business? Is it three shimmering blobs languishing on fluffy clouds and watching the world with a collective air of boredom or impotent anxiety?

The Scottish dance 'The Dashing White Sergeant' is a reel for sets of three often danced at weddings. A gentleman stands between two ladies, and opposite another lady who in turn is partnered by two gentlemen. The two sets bow to each other. Then they all hold hands to form one circle. Round for eight steps they dance, then back. Next the middle dancer of each set bows to and turns each partner. Then the set of three dance around one another forming a moving figure of eight. Finally the set of three take hands and approach the opposite set, say farewell to them with a yell and a stamp of feet and proceed to meet a new set of three to begin the reel again. The dance alternates between 'we are three', and 'we are one'. It is an exuberant reel with lots of laughter and greetings and stamping of feet.

For me the Trinity is like this exuberant dance of three; laughing, stamping, clapping as their bodies weave an ever-changing pattern. In fact the early Greek theologians when attempting to describe the Trinity used the word *perichoresis*. It means 'dancing around'. This loving, creative and passionate community of Divine Persons is the God to whom I address my longing for intimacy. I believe that sex too is a dancing around of three; my partner, myself and the Spirit of God.

What about you? Noticing how you feel and what you think about God is important. So take your time but don't worry if all that you can perceive when you try to picture God is a blank. Be assured you are not alone. A blank in the place of God may indicate that you experience God as beyond everything you know. This is an authentic spirituality. Or it may indicate that what the Church has offered in the way of theology and spirituality has made no connection with your own experience of life. God, not one to be stymied by the frailties of the Church, is still present to you even in the absence you may now feel.

Once you have spent some time reflecting on the Trinity consider Aelred's second point. How do you react to the image of Christ's presence in your bedroom? Perhaps it seems absurd. Perhaps it makes you feel uneasy. But play with the idea for a moment. If Christ truly is present, in what ways might he be making his presence known? When there is laughter . . . where is Christ? When there is physical delight . . . where is Christ? When there is climax . . . where then is Christ? And in times of disappointment, frustration, conflict . . . where is Christ? Surely not standing outside the door!

Certainly many people have experienced a profound spiritual dimension to sex; a transcendence that goes beyond the physical delight and emotional charge; a glimpse however fleeting of a reality beyond the self, the possibility of communion with the very Source of all Love. I'm not sure how many of us would immediately attribute this numinous experience to the presence of a third (albeit Divine) presence in the bed but perhaps we should.

Aelred's view of sex is more recently expressed by the author Lewis Smedes. Referring to Karl Barth's interpretation of the biblical story of creation – that in our sexuality we encounter the God-like in ourselves – Smedes (1993) wrote:

> Sexuality is the human drive toward intimate communion. Beyond the glandular impulse, the human sexual urge is always towards another person. We want to experience the other, to trust the other and be trusted by him, to enter the other's life by entering the vital embrace of his/her body. We need finally to experience the other in the rhythm of receiving and giving that can be felt in that passionate encounter called sexual intercourse.
>
> This is why sexuality is the sign and seal of God in our body-life. As bodies we experience the urge first in the vague sense of physical restlessness; as persons we experience it in the desire for a person. Here sexuality emerges as erotic desire. Sexual intercourse – at its best – is an epitome of the responsive life of persons in communion. Only in sexual communion, however, is there the added ingredient that makes it most exciting and dangerous: it is the ingredient of passion and ecstasy, the discarding of restraint and reserve. This is why it has the potential to be the epitome of communion: it involves the greatest amount of personal risk.

Smedes concludes that 'Our sexuality is, if not the essence as Barth suggests, at least a deep dimension of God-likeness'.

What might happen if we risk making a connection between the ecstasy we can enjoy beneath the sheets with our lover and the promise of communion with God that beats within our souls? If our drive towards intimacy with God affects and is affected by our drive towards intimacy with another person what are the possibilities for both? If both our sexuality and our spirituality are dimensions of the one longing for intimacy sown into our being by a most loving and relational God then at the very least I think we may expect to encounter the presence of Christ in our most intimate moments.

But before we go any further exploring connections between our relationship with partner and with God a word or two of caution is called for. The quest for intimacy requires a little faith and a measure of self-love in addition to the desire for it. Without these we are not ready to begin.

Life is difficult and living with another, even if we can find that person, is not an easy endeavour. All our most enduring love songs attest to the fact that the course of true love never runs smooth. Often we are left wondering if it is at all possible to realize the relationship we can envisage so clearly in our minds and hearts. What is more, while living with another person is difficult, living with the Living God can be even trickier.

Before we pursue a deeper intimacy with our partner we need to have a reasonable faith in the present quality of our relationship. We have to be able to trust, to some extent, our partner's loving intentions towards us whenever mistakes are made, misunderstandings occur, feelings are hurt and defensive barriers go up. If our faith in this relationship is at an all time low we would be foolish to begin praying for intimacy.

We cannot hope to find intimacy in a marriage that is

abusive or in a relationship that is at the point of break-ing under terrible strain. Intimacy is not yet a possibility in these situations. There is work to be done, perhaps with the help of a counsellor or priest. The grace we need at the present moment and in the present situation is not intimacy. It may be something like courage, or hope, or wisdom. In extreme cases it may be just too late for this particular relationship and the grace needed for both is to make a good end to it. Ignatius tells us to ask for what we need in the here and now. We need to resist the temptation to ask for a grace that lies a few graces ahead. This inclination to leap ahead is strong in all of us but it is not kind to ourselves nor is it conducive to a lasting intimacy.

We also need a measure of self-love: an attitude to our selves and our lives that is generally positive and grounded in a healthy, lived experience. Without this we will lack either the confidence and indeed the vital sense of humour needed to be open to the grace of intimacy, or the real and developed affective life which is the terrain of our quest. If I am struggling with a very low self-esteem or deep emotional wounds as yet unhealed that compel me to protect myself from further hurts and drive me into a life of fantasy, then this quest is not for me. Not yet.

What is the grace I really need now, at this moment of time and in these circumstances? It is unlikely to be inti-macy. It may be something lighter, like friendship, or it may be something quite deep, like forgiveness. It may be that I need the grace of freedom to seek the help and support I need to address my problems and seek their resolution or healing. The same cautions apply when we consider our relationship to God. Without faith in God's creative and loving intention for us and a measure of self-love we would be crazy to approach the Divine asking for an intimate encounter. To abandon myself entirely into God's hands, as Ignatius recommends, I must trust myself and my God. Neither can be taken for granted.

I often find myself saying to groups of people 'God is good; wholly good and only good.' Usually they nod earnestly but often they miss the point. In fact the more earnestly they nod the less they seem to grasp what I am saying. Some of my most earnest nodders, I have to tell you, have been groups of clergy. Surprising as it may seem, trust in a wholly good God can be elusive to even the most seasoned church person.

We all have notions of what God is like. They are pictures or images and are at best partial; they do not, cannot, contain the whole measure of God. Some of our images are not even accurate. But unfortunately this does not prevent them from being influential in our lives. J. B. Phillips gives several very useful descriptions of some popular but unhelpful pictures we can have of God. One of them is the Resident Policeman, and here is what Phillips (1952) says about it:

> This image is strong when God is experienced primarily through the voice of conscience. Conscience, of course, is not simply the voice of God – it is far more often the voice of our upbringing, leading us to feel today the way we were taught to feel as children.
>
> Many, however, can't distinguish between conscience and God. Accordingly, they feel themselves most aware of God when conscience is talking and making them feel bad. For them, God becomes a policeman waiting to catch them out in wrongdoing.

I have observed that for good Christian people, to leave behind some of their more familiar and unhelpful pictures of God can feel like unfaithfulness. These images of God, whether helpful or not, feel necessary to faith. Fear of losing faith holds people captive, prevents them from embarking on a quest for something more. Any suggestion that a picture of God could be dropped as unnecessary or unhelpful causes intense feelings of guilt often resulting in a harshness towards self and the one making the suggestion.

I recall one clergyman asking me, after a week of listening to my talk of a wholly good and only good God: 'Do I understand you to say that God is never disappointed?' Who told this man that God *could* be disappointed? Was it God? I doubt it. But wherever the message was heard and learned this man could now no longer conceive of encountering any other God. He expected God to be disappointed each time they met. This expectation would significantly affect his chances of an intimate relationship to God, but I guess that wasn't all bad news. There is always a pay-off with any of our pictures. I may find it easier to remain faithful to a god who can be disappointed by me than to conceive of God as the One who is never disappointed.

In the first case what actually disappoints my god can be discovered. Then the rules become clear and can be kept, more or less. When I make a mistake and disappoint myself and my god, I can ask for forgiveness. But if God is never disappointed then what am I to do with my many disappointments in myself and in others? Can you see the huge implications of a God who is never disappointed? For a start such a God would be up close, intimate; there would be no need for this God to keep a safe distance between us. It is we who distance ourselves from others due to our disappointment in them. We assume that God experiences disappointment as we do, and reacts in the same way. Can you feel the attraction to the notion of a smaller, more easily manageable deity who can be kept at arm's length?

If we are to encounter the one true God who is *more* we must, with God's grace, venture beyond our partial images. We must take up Ignatius' challenge to abandon ourselves into God's hands and wait there to be surprised, perhaps even scandalized, by what God intends to make of us.

Along with faith in the goodness of God we need a measure of self-love before we pray for intimacy with God. Unfortunately I meet very few praying Christians who actually love themselves at all. They may have images and pictures of God that are harsh and remote but the image they have of themselves is a million times worse. What use is it to pray for an intimate relationship with God if deep down you feel that no one, human or divine, could want any kind of relationship with you?

Ask for what you really do need. Before intimacy comes encounter. There is a new hymn written to an old tune that has the words: 'Will you love the "you" you hide if I but call your name?' (*Common Ground*, 1988). Perhaps you might seek the grace of this encounter with Jesus who calls you by name and already loves the hidden you.

Christians who do not love themselves find it hard and sometimes impossible to be good to themselves. In the 'Harry Potter' series of children's books Dobby, a house elf, is so used to being treated shabbily that he cannot accept the slightest kindness. Harry, being himself a kind boy, invites Dobby to sit down. The elf immediately goes and bangs his head against the wall to make recompense for enjoying this kindness.

I think I've met some Christians who feel and act the same way towards themselves. Perhaps you have too. For them following Jesus is all about self-denial and any notion of a pursuit of the gift of intimacy understandably sounds like out-and-out hedonism. It just seems so selfish; wanting something for oneself, contrary to the call to self-sacrifice that rings loudly around many churches. The quest for intimacy smacks to many of a Christianity disparagingly labelled as 'me and God'.

Certainly there is a real risk here. If we embark on a quest for intimacy with our partner we risk becoming the kind of couple so wrapped up in ourselves as to exclude all friends and family. If we pursue intimacy with God we risk becoming too heavenly minded to be any earthly good. We probably all know people who fall into either or both categories.

However, authentic and healthy intimacy does not result in obsession or exclusion. On the contrary, when we open up to intimacy with our partner, or with God, we find that all others are made more welcome in the space of our life. Intimacy is a grace that sits easily with us. It allows us to be relaxed and totally ourselves around our friends, family, colleagues. Everyone benefits from our playfulness, our confidence and our passion. Remember that intimacy with community proceeds from intimacy with partner and intimacy with God. Evidence of this is a reliable sign of the authenticity of our intimacy.

But I confess that when I dream, I dream of me. When

God dreams, God-in-me dreams of me; of my completion as a human being, made in the image of God. Refusing to dream the dream of intimacy is not selfless or wholesome, or righteous or generous. It's not even Christian. There is no way round it. We must take the risk and pray that God keeps us alert to the possibility of veering off towards hedonism!

Ignatius believed that we can find God in everything. Everything constituting the lived experience of our lives, that is. So we can encounter God in times of joy and in times of sorrow, not through any pious effort but through grace. In fact we, of necessity, must meet God within our own experience. We have nowhere else to go. We may go to church, but we will not find God there unless we *experience* church. How often do we make the effort to attend church and then merely spectate wondering later why our attendance never really touches us?

Contrast this with a group of teenagers at a pop concert. They do more than spectate. They shout and clap and sing, and scream and dance and hug each other, and throw flowers or underwear on to the stage. They sweat and laugh and cry, and come away saying 'What an awesome experience!' We might address them with the words of Jesus: 'Truly you are not far from the Kingdom of God.'

Or contrast it with your best memory of a night of passion with your partner. I am confident that you did more than spectate here. Again that experience of laughter, tenderness, urgency, sweat, power, surrender and much more brought you close to the Kingdom of God. Finding God in everything means we can indeed encounter God beneath the sheets. What a thought.

Now for most Christians personal prayer is likely to be

a part of our lived experience too and this offers a most fruitful encounter with God. However, turning up for prayer does not guarantee that we are seeking such an encounter, just as lying beneath the sheets with our partner does not always mean that we are disposed towards a night of energetic sex. We may just want to sleep. Assuming that we want to do more than sleep through our prayer it will be useful to practise the approach used by Ignatius and known as imaginative contemplation. So let us begin to seek the grace of intimacy with a simple contemplation of an enjoyable encounter in our own lives.

When I do this little exercise with groups I always caution them to look for a small episode. Life is difficult, sometimes crushingly so. Our good memories are moments rather than hours; is more likely to be one warm summer's day rather than the whole summer. The significant thing is this: a good memory stays good. No matter if it is surrounded in time by conflict or unhappiness, the memory keeps its goodness and is not affected by what went on before, or what transpires after it. Let me give you an example.

Seventeen years ago my husband and I had a holiday in mainland Greece. My good memory is of our first stroll from the hotel to the beach. It was six o'clock at night but the sun was hot on my back and as I sat on a rock, eyes closed, and listened to the water lapping gently at my feet I thought: 'Two weeks . . . I've got a whole two weeks of this.' I had been working all kinds of hours for a few months and so the thought of two weeks of complete relaxation was bliss. Now the next morning my husband and I had a huge argument, as often happens with couples at the start of a much-needed holiday. But the mess of that argument does not rob my good memory of any of its joy. When I close my eyes and allow my breathing to slow down a little, when I recall the sights and sounds and smells and textures of that scene on the beach, I can feel again the warm sun on my back and the gratitude in my heart.

Try it for yourself with the memory of an enjoyable encounter with your partner or with a close friend. It could be a walk you shared together, or a moment of laughter about something, or it could be that best-ever memory of sex. Contemplative use of our imagination is a God-given facility in each one of us but it is worth thinking of it as a muscle that may need toning up if it has fallen into disuse over the years. So be patient as you use this imaginative replay of a good memory to exercise your contemplative muscle. Gaze at the scene in a relaxed and leisurely manner and notice as much as you can. Use all your senses to reconstruct this joyful memory and notice too your feelings and emotions. Repeat the exercise of remembering now and then. Each time you may notice the same things as before or different things.

It can be very useful to keep a permanent record of the things that happen when we contemplate by jotting them down. Ignatius kept a journal and in it he recorded what happened, what he noticed, each time he prayed. God's revelation to us is gradual; if we keep a journal of our prayer we will be able to see, over a period of time, where God has been present in our ordinary life and what God has been saying to us.

So select an attractive plain-paper note book. Date the first page and resolve to write in this journal as to an intimate and completely confidential friend. If it helps, imagine that your friend is a prisoner of conscience in some impenetrable fortress. Your friend will by some profound providence receive each journal entry. To hear news of you is all that makes life worth living. So make each entry as honest and open as you can. This too is an encounter that holds the potential for intimacy.

Keep the journal and a pen handy as you work through this book. Take a little time at the end of a contemplative period to make a few notes, even a drawing or two, about what happened, how you felt, what you noticed, any surprises, and any questions you now have. Apart from using it to record the fruit of your contemplations you can jot down any thoughts, feelings, questions, strands of long-forgotten poetry, crazy dreams you remember from a night's sleep. All of these are precious treasures to your friend in the fortress so record anything you do not want to forget, even if the significance of an entry escapes you for the moment. Having bubbled up to the surface of your consciousness it *has* a significance. Jot it down.

You might usefully end each contemplation by asking yourself 'How do I feel?' and noting down your responses to this question. The quest for intimacy begins when we encounter our emotions and discover how we feel about our experience. It is part of the grace of being known, first by self, then by another. But we also want to know this other – this partner, this God – and in doing so we know ourselves still more deeply.

I believe that by turning contemplatively to Scripture we can satisfy both parts of our longing. In the following chapters we will contemplate some emotional encounters recorded in Scripture and also our own personal encounters with ordinary life and love. The gift of encounter, and the potential for intimacy are present to us in both. We only need to ask God for a deep awareness of this in each encounter of our day.

References

Common Ground. Edinburgh, Saint Andrew Press, 1988.

Empereur SJ, James L., *Spiritual Direction and the Gay Person*. London, Continuum, 1998.

Nelson, James, *The Intimate Connection*. London, SPCK, 1992.

Phillips, J. B., *Your God Is Too Small*. London, Epworth Press, 1952.

Smedes, Lewis, *Sex For Christians*. London, Triangle, 1993.

3

Come and See

Intimacy is an invitation.

First comes encounter, then an invitation is given and received: 'Come and see.' With it I invite you into the space of my life. You invite me into yours. We remain as two individuals but with respect and increasing levels of trust our souls begin to orbit. We make discoveries, want to know more. We linger, enjoy the warmth of this tentative relationship, find ourselves enriched by it. The invitation can be spontaneous or deliberate and either way the resulting intimacy will vary in degree and duration depending on circumstances and inclination.

Given space and inclination, intimacy grows. For me it is laughter that is loud and gives me an ache and is shared by my husband who gets the joke. It is skilled loving that sustains an edge of excitement and adventure to our daily living. And always (well nearly always) it is a passion that threatens to set the bed sheets on fire. Intimacy promises me all of these in addition to a mortgage, several noisy children and a mountain of ironing lurking in a cupboard waiting to jump out at the first person foolish enough to open the door. Of course life is a miracle!

Laughter, love and passion – doesn't that sound inviting? The good news is that God thinks so too. God is the one issuing the invitation. After all God created us for intimacy and desires intimacy with us; a relationship full of laughter, love and passion. It was God's intention that when I am in love I see love everywhere, feel love's creative power, know the rightness, the necessity of love for the completion of humanity made in God's image. Intimacy is an invitation to discover an ever-deepening and passionate mixture of *agape* and *philia* as well as *eros* and *epithymia*; universal love as well as particular love. There are very few of us who realize what this intimacy will make of us, our families, friends, and wider communities if only we could abandon ourselves into its hands and let ourselves be formed by its grace.

But if intimacy is an invitation it is sadly not one we are certain to accept. Within each of us there lurks a strong resistance to the invitation we are being extended. To know and be fully known by another person or by God requires that we grow spiritually, but

Spiritual growth demands much that we are unwilling to give. It threatens to loosen our cherished attachments, to change or even dissolve our frozen images of ourselves, and to reveal certain truths about ourselves that we are loath to admit. Further, it asks sacrifices of our time, energy and resources; it demands our very hearts. It should not be surprising to find ourselves resisting that which we consciously most desire, or distorting spiritual truth into self-contrived figments that we hope might give us fulfilment without sacrifice. (May, 1992)

The less we know and understand ourselves, the more frightening the prospect of such spiritual growth seems. So our desire to know and be known, though powerful, is also ambivalent. We want intimacy but we do not want it unconditionally. We are attached to our wealth, power, honour, or more simply to our peace and quiet, our privacy. We want intimacy but we do not want it to cost us the independence these possessions secure. And while intimacy is a gift, independence (the antithesis of intimacy) can be worked for or won, bought and sold and can always look glamorously attractive to our hungry eyes.

This enticing independence comes in a complete range of products: cars, computers, plastic surgery, personal development, a career, a new home, an exciting holiday, a healthy lifestyle. Even dog-food can be sold as a life-enhancing answer to all of our longing. Looking for intimacy, we are content to be sold sexy dog-food and turned into shop-aholics.

Addicted consumers are not the most reflective of people. There is no time for honest soul-searching when one is hunting for a bargain in the wealth, power and honour departments of life. No time for other people either and these are encountered in the daily rush as commodities to be moved around, used, discarded.

Who will deliver us from our ambivalent and driven selves? At one time it was believed that psychotherapy would. The observations of Freud and those who followed him promised to cure the troubled souls of a modern people determined to slough off the biblical notion of sin as necessary to any understanding of human behaviour and experience.

Studying both, Freud posited that the human personality is a balancing act between the id, the ego and the superego. Present at birth, the id holds all our most primeval instincts, impulses and desires. It is, according to Freud, totally selfish, insisting on instant fulfilment of any desire. In childhood the ego begins to develop and tries to satisfy the appetites of the id in a reasonable and practical way, taking into account the realities of the world. Then there is the superego. The superego is a bit like an internalized version of our parents and other influential adults. It develops throughout childhood and is with us, like a resident policeman, throughout adulthood. The superego, like the id, must be kept in check by the balancing ego because it is strongly authoritarian and can often make unreasonable and unhealthy demands on the person. Between these two and the experiences of life we are all likely to develop some at least mildly neurotic tendencies and culturally developed prejudices. Freud believed that coping with these can lead to repression and to a negative self-image that paralyses some part of our potential.

A useful enough theory as far as it goes. It may well explain why our genius for intimacy fails to realize its true potential in our lives and relationships. However, we are still left with a problem.

In general, psychotherapy hopes to encourage more efficient living, and its values and intentions often reflect those that prevail in the culture at any given time. For example, psychotherapy often seeks to bolster an individual's capacity to gratify needs and desires and to achieve a sense of autonomous mastery over self and circumstances. Both of these orientations are quite prominent in modern society as a whole. (May, 1992)

But intimacy requires that we do more than cope efficiently with our inner world of appetites, desires and standards. Intimacy proclaims liberation from our paralysis. It insists that we enjoy life in all its fullness. Intimacy is a grace while efficient living is a compromise that leaves us still longing for something *more*.

Paul, in his letter to the Romans, knew nothing of neurosis, the superego or the id. However, he knew the workings of his inner self; the attraction and resistance he experienced to God's love:

It happens so regularly that it's predictable. The moment I decide to do good, sin is there to trip me up. I truly delight in God's commands, but it's pretty obvious that not all of me joins in that delight. Parts of me covertly rebel, and just when I least expect it, they take charge. (Peterson, 1993)

Is it not the same for all of us? The good we long to do is part of God's grace and our genius. Sin is our covert resistance to this grace and therefore to God. We long for intimacy but part of us covertly rebels, choosing independence and coping strategies as the easier options.

The resulting lack of intimacy with God and our neighbour is cosmic in significance because it allows us to remain untouched by either the joy or the suffering of others. It lies at the root of every war, famine and man-made disaster. Lack of intimacy results in the collapse of family and community while it fosters fascism, bigotry and all other forms of isolationism that are attempts to resist the uncompromising love of God. Lack of intimacy builds bombs, cuts down forests, makes refugees of entire nations. As human beings sharing a small and vulnerable planet at the start of the third millennium lack of intimacy is now our greatest danger. It is our sin.

God knows that sin is not immorality but independence. Our salvation does not lie in a morally acceptable life but in an acceptance of God's invitation to love and be loved, know and be known, by a human partner if we are fortunate to have one, by the circles of community that make up our lives, and most crucially by the Creator of all love and knowledge. Fortunately God is not leaving the pursuit of intimacy either to us or to our psychotherapists. You may find much that agrees with the ideas of this book in the bestselling self-help book *The Art of Loving* by Erich Fromm. However, you will also discover that while he emphasizes the need for individuals and society to develop and practise the art of love Fromm discounts God from the picture. It is a crucial difference and for me a fatal flaw.

Before ever you were aware of yourself as a separate human soul God desired you. God is the One in passionate pursuit of us, the beloved. And God is stronger than any superego, id, neurosis or prejudice. God is a lover adept at seduction, pursuing with optimistic passion: unafraid, wearing heart on sleeve and supremely confident of love's eventual conquest. This quest is primarily God's love affair, not yours. We can co-operate with God's quest and begin to perceive what intimacy might make of us by turning to a passage of Scripture that describes an encounter followed by an invitation.

Now when we contemplate Scripture we use our

imagination to replay the scene we have read as though it were a video. It is good to read the passage over slowly a few times. Read it out loud and with expression. I think the stories of Scripture have more impact when read aloud. Try reading it in different styles: with incredulity as though the story is hard to accept or understand, then in a whisper, or confidently, or even tearfully if the passage lends itself to this. If you have used the same version of Scripture for many years you will be surprised by the freshness a new version can offer. Try it for yourself.

When you have read the passage several times, familiarizing yourself with it, put the Bible down and prepare to gaze with your imagination at the scene you have just read. Close your eyes and begin to set the scene in your own way. Use your own storehouse of memories to paint the pictures. Some people find it useful to think of themselves as a film director and the gospel story as a scene to be directed. It may not strike you as a very reverential approach to take to Scripture, but it works. It can also be useful to question your own senses. What do I see? What do I hear? What can I smell, taste? What am I touching or what is touching me?

Our passage is found at John 1.35–39:

On the following day as John stood there with his disciples, Jesus passed, and John stared hard at him and said, 'Look, there is the lamb of God'. Hearing this, the two disciples followed Jesus. Jesus turned round, saw them following and said, 'What do you want?' They answered, 'Rabbi' – which means Teacher – 'where do you live?' 'Come and see' he replied; so they went and saw where he lived, and stayed with him the rest of that day. It was about the tenth hour.

The two men are not sure exactly why they are following Jesus. They do not yet know what it is they are looking for. So when asked, they answer with a question – 'Where do you live?' The invitation is given immediately and unreservedly – 'Come and see'. The encounter has lasted for only seconds but already Jesus pursues the grace of intimacy. He invites them to come and see where he lives, how he spends his day, what is important to him. He offers an invitation to intimate knowledge of himself and straight away they sense this is the answer to their searching. They accept the invitation and go with him.

Try to set the scene of the passage. You may imagine the hills behind Jerusalem, but equally validly you may set the scene in the streets of your home town. Trust your own imagination and play a little with it. Once you have set the scene you can try to imagine the action and dialogue. You may view this from the sidelines, as a narrator or director would, or you may play with the idea of being in the scene; a disciple perhaps, or Jesus himself. Ignatius found this role-taking to be very fruitful and discovered that contemplation became prayer as he began to listen with new ears to the things Jesus said, and even approached to ask his own questions of Jesus.

Here are some hints to help your contemplation of this short passage. Imagine you are the disciple hearing John's words: 'Look, there is the lamb of God.'

⋏ What thoughts and feelings arise within you?
⋏ What makes you leave John's side and follow after Jesus?
⋏ How do you feel when he turns and spots you?
⋏ What motivates your question 'Where do you live?'

⋏ 'Come and see'. How does this reply affect you? What are your hopes? Fears?

⋏ How inclined are you to accept this stranger's invitation?

When we contemplate a gospel passage our imagination fleshes out the story with the thoughts and feelings, the hopes and fears, of the characters involved. Remember to jot down whatever occurs to you.

One passage from Scripture can be imagined several times and from different viewpoints; here are some guiding questions to help you gaze at the scene from Jesus' perspective.

⋏ What are you thinking about as you walk along that day?

⋏ How do you become aware of the two men following you?

⋏ What do you see as you look into their faces?

⋏ What effect has their question 'Where do you live?' have on you?

⋏ What are you hoping for when you issue the invitation 'Come and see'?

With a little practice if this is new to you other questions will present themselves. And since God is good and since the Word of God is alive and actively breathing into our life we discover, as Ignatius did, that praying contemplatively with Scripture affects us. Gradually our hearts and minds are affected as we encounter Jesus in a new and more personal way. As we 'Come and see' where Jesus lives in our lives and what he is about, we find our attraction to him growing.

Imagine that Jesus sees you as you walk through an ordinary day. The Spirit within Jesus points to you, just as John did in the passage, and says 'Look, there is the child of God.' Imagine that Jesus, hearing this prompting within him, follows after you and that you become aware of this. You turn and ask Jesus what he wants. Hear his reply 'Where do you live?' and then issue the invitation 'Come and see'. Then you might, in your imagination, replay a 24-hour period with the sense of Jesus gazing at it with you. He has come to see where intimacy is in your life. Look with Jesus for laughter, and love and passion, for times when you feel most truly alive. Just notice what Jesus notices. Don't judge or try to analyse. Simply notice the moods, colours, feelings, thoughts. Then you might ask Jesus something. Perhaps 'What do you want?' Listen to any reply that seems to come and notice how it makes you feel.

These are only three examples of what you might do given a leisurely gazing at this passage with your own imagination. Do not be afraid to experiment with others that occur to you. Just do not attempt them all at once. Contemplation is good, but nothing is good in excess! All of the suggestions for contemplation in this book can be repeated as often as you find useful. Ignatius knew that it was important not to rush with prayer. He often advocated that one contemplation be repeated as often as it yielded fruit. So do not leave this passage from John's Gospel in a hurry. If you have the time it would be useful to contemplate it for about half an hour each day for three or four days.

In addition each morning as you rise from bed invite Jesus to 'Come and see' the day with you. This may take some time to establish itself in your early morning routine, so don't be discouraged by the number of days that you rise and forget to issue the invitation. Just do it whenever you remember in the day. Then at night as you prepare to sleep you might take a few minutes to look over the day and notice what it was that Jesus saw with you, what the hours disclosed about you and about the presence or absence of intimacy in your life. Then you might again invite Jesus to come and see, this time where you live in your dreams.

'Come and see.' It is an invitation to intimacy. Extending it to Jesus is a form of prayer. I think you will find it an efficacious one. But what might happen if we begin also to extend this invitation to our partner? When the day's work is done and any children or pets are fed, watered and settled for the night, two people who desire to co-operate with God's grace of intimacy might well take 20 minutes over a coffee or a brandy to share the day with each other. The invitation I extend to my partner is to come and see with me what the day has been. Not just the facts and feelings of it. I invite him to help me explore the deeper meaning and movements. My partner offers me the gift of deep attentiveness. Later I will reciprocate when he explores his experience of the day.

He listens to me and asks a useful question here and there to facilitate further reflection. The quality of the listening and the questions is vital. Two people who live long together can gradually develop a way of half-listening to each other. Since we know the other well we do not expect to hear anything new. While we think we are listening to what is actually being said, now we are really paying more attention to things said and understood, or misunderstood, many times before. The one sharing senses this and inevitably takes an imperceptible step back from intimacy.

But if my partner can come to this encounter expecting to meet a me as yet undiscovered, then the quality of his listening will be quite different. It will encourage me to further reflective disclosure, will nurture intimacy between us. A good question shows that he has been listening and desires to facilitate my exploration. A good question is open and kind. It rarely begins: 'Don't you think . . .?' or 'Surely . . .?, or 'Yes, but . . .?' A good question is not a thinly veiled attempt to correct my perception or redirect me or hijack the focus from my experience to his. So good questions can be:

⋏ 'How did that feel?'
⋏ 'What seems significant about that meeting/incident/ emotion/inclination?'
⋏ 'Do you know what you were hoping for then? And now?'

Good questions rarely if ever begin with the word 'Why . . .?' Perhaps it is a form of interrogation overused in many relationships at home, work, in politics, play and even in church and not always kindly meant. It can be a cold shower to the possibility of intimacy. I wonder why.

Could it be that often there is no satisfactory answer to the question 'Why?' Why do I feel the way I do? Why did I do the thing I did? Why am I happy/sad/confident/ afraid? Why is life difficult? Why do bad things happen to good people? Why natural disasters? Well, why not?

'Why' is a question asked most usefully by infants and

by scientists. It looks for absolutes, certainties, concrete answers *now*. Children of course require some certainties in their lives if they are not to grow into neurotic adults; for them the question 'Why?' is a tool of discovery. Scientists too use this tool and with it they discover not *why* the universe is but *how* it is and how it works. But once we are grown and, excepting the field of science, certainty and absolutes need to give way to mystery. The 'Why' and 'Why not' approach to life will no longer serve all our needs and longings. When we are grown there are other, more fruitful questions waiting. These questions often begin with the word 'What'.

Several times in the gospels Jesus asks someone '*What* is it you want me to do for you?' In the passage we are presently contemplating he asks the two disciples of John: '*What* do you want?' and addressing his own closest companions he asks 'Do you know *what* I have done to you?' These are good questions that facilitate and encourage intimate disclosure while offering attentive listening and unconditional acceptance. We will turn our contemplative gaze on them later in this book. For now I would observe that intimacy never begins in the bedroom but can easily be sabotaged there by the questions 'Why?' and 'Why not?'

Intimacy begins with encounter and deepens with an invitation to disclosure. Exciting as it undoubtedly can and should be to reveal our bodies to another it is even more erotic to reveal our most secret desires. This disclosure can begin as we move around one another in the limited space of our home, work, community of friends and family. It continues and deepens over this cup of coffee, these attentive questions and this daily discovery and exploration of each other. From there it feels like the most natural thing in the world to invite my partner to 'Come and see' who I am, what I feel, what I want. To discover where I live as we move to an encounter with one another, and with the God of intimacy, beneath the sheets.

References

Fromm, Erich, *The Art of Loving*. London, Harper Collins, 1995.

May, Gerald G., *Care of Mind, Care of Spirit*. New York, Harper Collins, 1992.

Peterson, Eugene, *The Message*. Colorado, NavPress Publishing Group, 1993.

4

They Have Run Out of Wine

Intimacy is a bit like wine.

Given quality grapes grown in rich soil and ripened by the sun a good wine should result. But it takes time, a little agricultural effort, some skill and probably no small measure of luck. On our quest for the wine of intimacy we provide the time and effort in pursuit of the grace by turning up for prayer. God generously provides the skill and the divine luck when we do: what we call grace and providence.

If intimacy is like wine then people are surely like grapes. We take time to ripen or mature. The same wisdom that assures us the best things in life are and always will be free also testifies to the fact that mature life truly does begin at around 40. This maturity combines the skills and confidence that come from having lived through a few decades and the ability to reflect on that experience, with a playfulness that is our appropriate inheritance from childhood. It also comes with love handles and squidgy tummy muscles. With all of these we are at last ready to reap the benefits of those years we have spent growing up. We feel with Browning that 'the best is yet to be'. Now is the season in which to produce a vintage intimacy both with God and with our partner.

Sadly, long before we reach the maturity that will provide the right conditions for intimate union with God something goes awry for many of us. Instead of ripening we become bruised by life. Our hopes are blighted by the storms or the exhausting round of daily responsibilities and chores just dries up some vital sap within us. Along the way life has become more of an endurance test than an exciting gift, and we have become content merely to last the course rather than live the adventure of it. And it all seems so normal.

No matter to what extent this has happened we will find help in the contemplation of a story of wine recorded in John 2.1–10:

> Three days later there was a wedding at Cana in Galilee. The mother of Jesus was there, and Jesus and his disciples had also been invited. When they ran out of wine, since the wine provided for the wedding was all finished, the mother of Jesus said to him, 'They have no wine.' Jesus said, 'Woman, why turn to me? My hour has not come yet.' His mother said to the servants, 'Do whatever he tells you'. There were six stone jars standing there, meant for the ablutions that are customary among the Jews: each could hold twenty or thirty gallons. Jesus said to the servants, 'Fill the jars with water' and they filled them to the brim. 'Draw some out now' he told them 'and take it to the steward.' They did this; the steward tasted the water, and it had turned into wine. Having no idea where it

came from – only the servants who had drawn the water knew – the steward called the bridegroom and said, 'People generally serve the best wine first, and keep the cheaper sort till the guests have had plenty to drink; but you have kept the best wine till now.'

This is a lovely passage for contemplation. There cannot be many of us who have not been present at a wedding celebration or an anniversary party. The memories are unforgettable and can be drawn on to compose the sights, sounds, smells, textures and tastes of this scene.

So imagine the wedding at Cana, and enjoy yourself. It is a celebration with music and laughter, dancing and chatter, sunshine and fragrant flowers, with good food, and flowing wine. So indulge. Allow this contemplation to relax, revive and refresh you as the wedding party no doubt did for Jesus. Dance with him; a waltz, a barn dance, a passionate tango or an exuberant Jewish circle dance. Dance and laugh and remember what life feels like when it courses through your body.

After a while notice Mary, the mother of Jesus. She seems concerned, and you draw closer as she approaches her son. Hear her whisper in his ear: 'They have run out of wine.' Reflect for a moment on Mary's compassion for the young couple, her distress at the thought of anything spoiling their special day. They have run out of wine. She would not have it so, and she knows her son can help. He can help you too. Sometimes we become like a celebration that has run out of wine. In fact this wedding at Cana and your imaginative joining of it may have brought sharply into focus the painful contrast between your dreams and the present reality of your life and situation.

So quietly approach Jesus, as Mary did. Speak to him

of the way or ways in which your life has run out of wine. Feel your own distress as you notice how the gift of your life is in danger of being spoiled. Or notice how normal it seems to have run out of the things that formerly flavoured and spiced your life, and ponder whether or not this is as it should be. Ask Jesus to transform your sorrow or your apathy about this, the water of tears, into wine. Ask for a grace.

Though Jesus seems unsure, Mary is confident and tells the servants: 'Do whatever he tells you' (John 2.6). What Jesus instructs them to do is fill six large stone jars with water. It would be quite demanding physical work needing co-operation between the servants. It seems they went about the task enthusiastically for they 'filled them to the brim'.

We have a phrase: 'A lot of water has flowed under the bridge since then'. It refers to the events, joys, sorrows that make up the years of life and flow past without us ever being able to stop them. So now, like an obedient servant, do as Jesus advises. Take some time and expend some effort to collect as much of this water from your own river of life, even if it takes six 30-gallon jars to hold it all.

You might imagine that you are sitting on the grassy bank of a flowing river. Sit relaxed, breathe slowly, imagine the river, listen to the sound of it, trail your hand in the flowing waters and tell God in prayer that you want to collect the memories that make up this flow, ask for help. Gaze into the water until a memory breaks the surface. Collect this memory in your water jar by simply replaying it in your imagination with all its sights and sounds and tastes and textures and smells. Notice the effect the scene, incident, encounter had on you in the past and what effect it has today. Some memories are joyful, some are sad. That's life. We want Jesus to transform both into a celebration: into wine. When you are ready to move on return to gazing at the water, waiting for another memory to bubble up to the surface.

You could use your journal to record the process of collection. Whenever a memory comes to mind write it on your journal page. Just a word, or phrase or even a sketch: enough to capture the memory. Now you can have that good long look at it. Whenever we decide to take a leisurely look at something we are right back to that passage at the beginning of John, and that invitation of Jesus to 'Come and see'. The attentiveness and useful questioning we used with that passage will help our gazing now. Remember to explore the possibility of turning a 'Why?' question into a 'What?' one and exploring these fully. What does this memory tell me about myself, my life, my hopes? What am I aware of feeling now as I recall the memory? If this memory, whether sad or happy, holds a message of hope for me now – what would that message be?

Inevitably some of our memories will be of people who have left our life permanently but who were once an important part of it. Assuming the contribution they made was positive we might ask: 'What would that friend/parent/grandparent, etc. say to me now? What hope would he/she be holding in his/her heart for me?' I believe we all have a company of saints encompassing us and cheering us on, rooting for us, hoping passionately that we discover the best wine.

Of course, some memories may feature people whose

presence in our life was destructive. Be hospitable to these memories. Since God is good and wills to recreate good from even the worst of our experience they can also be useful. What might happen if I make a truce with these memories, accepting them as part of my life and seeking to make them my ally, rather than my enemy or recurring nightmare?

In the Second World War Italy fought on both sides at different times. She began as Britain's enemy, then changed her allegiance and fought with Britain against Germany and her allies. I suppose Britain could have rejected Italy's decision to change sides but what purpose would that have served? It made good sense to allow this change of allegiance but I doubt if relations were particularly warm between the two nations. Similarly it is possible to permit a hurtful or damaging incident to work for us in the present, even though it worked so determinedly against us in the past. We do not need to pretend gratitude for the incident, it is enough to co-operate thankfully with God who most lovingly seeks to recreate something good from it. What might God be hoping to recreate from the memory of that encounter or relationship or conflict?

Recreating takes time. This gathering and contemplation of all the water that has flowed under the bridge may take a few days. Each time you have space simply return to the river in your imagination and gaze at the water, journal at the ready. Once you feel the labour of collecting this personal water is complete leave the river and return to the wedding party.

At Cana, once the water was collected the hard work was over. All the servants were asked to do now was to

68

draw out some water and take it to the steward for tasting. Jesus did not even touch the water. He did not need to. 'Through him all things came to be, not one thing had its being but through him' (John 1.3). The essence of this water was already known to the Son. Its mystery fully understood. So the servants draw a pitcher of water and go looking for the man in charge. Somewhere between that drawing and the tasting a transformation takes place. The steward is impressed.

One of the useful things about imaginative contemplation is the way we can take one role and then another in the same scene. So far we have been the young couple and the servants. Now it is time to contemplate the steward. The important thing about this particular steward was that he had no hidden agendas or powerful prejudices. He was free to taste the wine and express his true and unambiguous opinion. The wine was excellent. Had he been secretly the enemy of the young couple the steward may have offered only grudging praise. Or he may even have sought to cast aspersions on the source of this wine: was it perhaps stolen? No such prejudices affected him. He was unbiased and therefore his opinion was dependable. We read that the amazed steward, having no idea where the wine came from sought out the lucky bridegroom and exclaimed with the enthusiasm of a connoisseur: 'People generally serve the best wine first, and keep the cheaper sort till the guests have had plenty to drink; but you have kept the best wine till now' (John 2.10).

Recently my family and I were on holiday in Florida and enthusiastically visited Disneyworld. At Epcot I discovered that all the water that exists on earth today is all the water that has ever existed. I found the simplicity of this fact stunning and spent the rest of my holiday watching reverently the gallons of water being used in the theme parks alone. Later I continued to ponder. The water in my body has been from the beginning. It is the same as that water over which God's spirit hovered at the dawn of creation. The tears of my life; tears of joy, tears of frustration, tears of grief, anger, fear, laughter and even those caused by hayfever: all of them are part of that one water that has always existed. The tears I shed today have been shed before by countless others. Only the present meaning of them is different.

This life of ours, like the water of creation and like the water at Cana, is already intimately known and understood by the Son. How could it be other? All things came into being through him. The Christ has already touched the essence of our life with his transforming and self-giving love (*agape*) and desire for communion (*eros*); all that is left for us to do is taste and see. I think Jesus understood this as only one who was there at creation can understand. Water, wine, both the same, from the one source, differing only in meaning. Water is the source of life. Wine the celebration of it. And life should always be celebrated.

So the steward sips the wine and his palate celebrates its quality. We too are called by love to celebrate the quality of our own life and this celebration will reinvigorate and surprise us with new possibilities for it. Sipping the wine we will discover that we are fearfully and wonderfully made. It is a discovery we need to make on our quest for intimacy with partner and with God.

However, we may not be as unbiased about our lives as the steward at Cana was about the wine. Our inner steward, that voice of conscience, code, set of standards, tester of experience, has its limitations. Life has inflicted some damage on us all and although we have some wisdom and facility for discernment we also have many fears and prejudices. This can mean that while a part of us welcomes the prospect of transformation in our life, another part dreads it.

Fortunately Jesus neither shrinks away from our damage nor writes us off because of it. There is a lovely passage in Isaiah that Matthew's Gospel applies to Jesus: 'He does not break the crushed reed, nor quench the wavering flame' (Isaiah 42.3). Instead, just as he wanted the steward at Cana to be the first to taste and approve what he had done with the water, so Jesus invites us to accept the reality of our life, recognize our fears and, subduing them by grace, welcome his transformation of them.

So take some time to ponder the question: What are these fears in me that might resist change and sabotage transformation in and of my life? Perhaps the idea of making an ally of one of my most painful memories of betrayal is unthinkable. Something in me resists this way forward. It seems frightening and I choose instead to water the memory with my bitter tears and watch it grow.

What grace do I require to subdue my fears? The realization that Jesus trusts himself and us is itself a grace. It can free us to look at our life and experience it in a new way. We witness the most surprising transformation take place as we allow the presence of Christ to effect a change, not in the facts of our lives but rather a change in the meaning and significance of events, choices, accidents, plans and relationships.

This whole contemplation can be repeated with the

focus on our marriage or partnership. After all it was the newly married couple who had run out of wine. If it is easy for one individual to run out of the enthusiasm, courage, dreams that once were important, how much more likely that a couple who set off on a journey together will experience weariness and disillusionment as the routine of daily living squeezes out the sense of adventure? Remember Mary's compassion: 'They have no wine' (John 2.4).

In what ways has your own marriage or partnership run out of wine? Try to name them. Don't think too much, just write down the words and phrases that present themselves to you. You are not writing them in stone. If any need changing or deleting on consideration you can score out.

Now collect some memories of this marriage – the water that has flowed under the bridge. You could plot the journey of your relationship through its anniversaries. Take a large sheet of paper and in the top left-hand corner draw a picture or write a phrase that captures the memory of the day you met. Now draw a path from this day to your first anniversary together. Draw or sketch with words this memory too. Continue, perhaps making the path itself reflect the ups and downs of your life together, the valleys and mountain-tops, the dangerous floods you have passed through, the lush pastures you have enjoyed. When the journey is complete become aware of your response to this little exercise in remembering. Then take some time to guide Jesus along the path, describing each part of the journey, asking him questions, allowing him to question you.

Another approach would be to use photo albums,

gazing at the photographs of yourself and partner in the early days of your relationship. Then look at your wedding photos, holiday snaps, birthdays, anniversaries. The arrivals of children are usually well recorded photographically and these provide a very useful way of getting in touch with our moods and feelings and hopes and fears over five, ten, twenty, even fifty years. Look at the eyes, the smiles and frowns. Re-member, literally put together again the day each photo was taken, and feel again the way you felt then. Gaze at each photo with Jesus, seeing them through his eyes, looking for intimacy and the absence of intimacy, the desire for intimacy, the frustration of that desire. Observe the ambivalence within.

We can ask the question: What fears in me might resist change or transformation in and of my marriage? What grace do I need to subdue my fears, free me from bias and allow me to embrace transformation? And an additional and extremely important question: How might my partner play a part in these graces?

Marriage is a mystery of life. A man and a woman leave their families and become one flesh, one kin, in the sight of God. At a Western wedding the party often begins with the groom and bride taking to the dance floor on their own to dance the first waltz together. It is a good illustration of the start of a marriage. Both families are present as witnesses and as a company of saints praying for this young couple. The man and woman step out from their own families and meet in the middle of the dance floor. They hold each other lightly and begin to move together to the music. They may not dance very elegantly together yet, they have much to learn both about the timing and steps of a good waltz and about the timing and steps of a good marriage. Other couples join them on the floor and these are often more experienced partners who dance together with an effortless fluidity delightful to watch.

Dance is an excellent metaphor, not only for the Trinity but for a marriage. When we dance it is clear that my partner's steps, sense of timing and ear for music can and do affect how we dance together. If one partner in a dance changes the pattern, adds something or removes something, then the other dancer must reciprocate or the two will be clumsily out of time, feet will be trodden on and arms will be jerked. We must agree the kind of dance we are attempting – fox-trot, waltz, quick-step, tango – if we are to avoid disaster and probable personal injury. It is the same for the dance of marriage. If I begin to allow Jesus to transform my life and experience I am going to move differently in the space of my marriage. Unless my partner is sensitive to this change of rhythm and movement in me and willing to be himself changed by it, we will come to a grinding halt in a very few bars. We must learn the new timing, patterns, steps together if we are to flow through life as one flesh, dance the one dance.

Therefore it will be very fruitful to approach Jesus together and make Mary's observation: we have run out of wine. Look through the photo albums together and explore together the memories and the feelings they arouse now. Listen to each other as you ponder the questions: what has changed, what has remained the same, what needs to change, what needs to be allowed to grow? How do we dance together and how do we long to dance together?

One question may remain in your mind as it does in

74

mine: Why did Jesus hesitate at his mother's request? John tells us it was because he was unsure that the timing was right for such a direct and noticeable sign of the Kingdom's immanence. Perhaps it also seemed untimely and unwise to interfere in the delicate relationship of a newly married couple. Once done the transformation of water into wine would not easily be undone. Whatever came from it was outwith the control of Jesus. It might cause more trouble than it resolved.

Imagine that the original wine for the party had been the gift of the groom's favourite uncle. Then this new wine, a gift it seems from the bride's Aunt Mary and her son, might cause ructions between relatives. Everyone who has ever planned a wedding knows how delicate the arrangements are made by the necessity not to offend any of the large group of usually overly-sensitive well-wishers. Perhaps Jesus knew only too well that fools rush in where angels fear to tread.

Similarly, Jesus will not willy-nilly transform your life or partnership without an explicit and informed petition from you. He needs to know you really want this done. That you understand that once done it cannot be undone. That you have counted the cost of transformation and of intimacy. Because there is a cost involved.

A cheap or simple wine does not demand much of the consumer, neither from his purse nor his palate. The best wines however are more complex, subtle, requiring of respect. They cannot be thrown in the refrigerator for a month and then cracked open to drink with a cheese dip. They need to be stored carefully, opened and allowed to breathe. They demand to be accompanied by the most tender of meats or the freshest of fish.

It is a similar story with marriage. In a mediocre marriage I am content to assume that my partner is the same yesterday, today and tomorrow. The same, that is, as my image of him. For I have an image of my husband. I know this image; it is familiar to me. He was never the same as my image of him, it could never contain the whole truth of him. He is other than I know or understand. This is okay. What makes married life mediocre and downright difficult is my insistence that my partner live up (or down) to my image of him. It certainly saves me a lot of effort if he does this; I do not have to expend time or energy discovering the man who is present to me now. Instead I can assume I know his tastes, opinions, dreams, sorrows. I can settle for an inferior vintage.

We need to remember and acknowledge that marriage has not always been treated with the respect it deserves. Marriage or its social equivalent has been a form of property control, slavery, social control, legalized prostitution. Most commonly nowadays it is a useful socio-economic unit for governments and markets, a mutual convenience once the bloom of romance has rubbed off, or a troublesome impediment soon to be got rid of – none of which can yield much grace but neither do any demand much respect.

Intimacy is a far superior wine to any of these. It is the best. You cannot contain this delicious and sophisticated wine in any old wineskin of a marriage. It is costly, requiring courage and skill and good taste on the part of both partners. So let us seek the graces that will allow our lives to accommodate the new intimacy. Let us taste and see that the Lord of creation and the wine of intimacy is very good.

5

Do You Know What I Have Done to You?

Intimacy is not the same as familiarity.

We can be very familiar with a person and yet not be at all intimate. All too often married couples become tediously familiar with one another without enjoying any depth of intimacy. Similarly many Christians are familiar with God but would not comprehend the possibility of intimacy with God.

Familiarity is safe. Intimacy can be dangerous. Familiarity has no unanswered questions while intimacy is full of them. In fact as intimacy deepens the more aware we become of all that is still unknown about the body, mind and soul of the loved one. This awareness serves to inflame our passion. The last shreds of familiarity give way to mystery and the facts we know about this other are obliterated by the light of our experience of him or her.

Prayerfully pursuing the grace of intimacy, embracing mystery and letting go of familiar kinds of knowledge in our personal relationship involves risk. It is what Erich

Fromm calls 'a daring plunge into the experience of union'. Being with another is daring. How I speak, act, express myself; these communications cause a reaction in the other. The risk here is that the reaction I cause is not the one I am hoping or intending or even meaning to produce. A gesture, a look, a sigh, can all be misinterpreted; received with a meaning and significance I did not intend, could not conceive.

So intimate relationships are risky. When it comes to intimacy of mind or body with our partner we may often feel a bit like the male praying mantis gingerly approaching the female with the intention of mating. She will either accept his advances or she will kill him. One wrong move and the hopeful mate is lunch.

Paradoxically however, if there is no sense of risk in an encounter then there is not likely to be much intimacy either. If everything I do and say and suggest to my partner is familiar to both of us then there is little risk of misunderstanding but even less chance of intimacy. Intimacy is a going beyond the known into the unknown. If couples understood this there would be more love affairs within marriage and committed partnerships and significantly fewer outside them.

If intimacy with a human and clearly visible partner whose tone of voice, choice of words and body language can all be attended to holds the risk of misinterpretation then intimacy with God who is beyond our five senses must present even more risks. In both cases our knowledge can only be finite and imperfect. We need to move beyond this knowledge *about* the other to embrace experiential knowledge *of* the other. Mystical union awaits us.

If truth were told however, mystical union is something

most of us are happy to leave to the mystics. Not so Jesus, which probably explains why he was so strikingly different from any other teacher in living memory of the crowds who listened to him. Here was a man who claimed not only to yearn for intimacy with the Creator, an original enough desire, but one who claimed to actually enjoy this intimacy to the full.

Now it was par for the course that a 'messiah' figure appearing to the people of Israel at the time would claim to have a special relationship with God. They all felt sure that they knew God's plan for the delivery of Israel, and had been sent or commissioned by God to carry it out. But the claim of Jesus was different to anything that had been heard before: 'The Father and I are one' (John 10.30). This was either lunacy or blasphemy, it couldn't possibly be true. Yet ever since he made the claim there have always been people who sensed that Jesus spoke the truth – those who experienced like the disciples some kind of felt knowledge of the unity of Father and Son. It was an experience that convinced them that he was and is intimately united with the Father and his mission as Messiah was and is to draw all of us into this same intimacy. This mission holds the same risks for Christ now as it did when he first spoke of vines and branches and the yield of good grapes and issued the invitation: 'Make your home in me, as I make mine in you' (John 15.4).

The risk for Christ and for us is not just that we cannot be bothered with such intimacy or are too fearful to take the plunge. It is simply that we are prone to misunderstanding and misinterpretation. Intimacy with Christ or with our partner is made difficult when one misunderstanding leads to another and another until a molehill grows into a mountain and there is no way over or round it. The mountain stands in the way and too often the hard work of tunnelling through is not an attractive prospect and seems to offer little reward. Prevention is usually better than cure. The way to avoid creating a mountain range in our marriage, partnership or faith is to reflect on this question often: 'Do you understand what I have done to you?' (John 13.12).

We need to tell each other how we have received and interpreted a look, a word, an action, and we need to do this often. It is a good addition to the 'Come and see' cup of coffee or brandy at the end of a busy day. On especially busy days the risk of misinterpretation between partners is at its greatest. If we only have a hurried half-hour together then what happens in that short time has a significance far out of proportion to its duration. Mistakes are made out of haste or preoccupation with the next task that looms before us and we overlook the signs in our partner that tell us some word or gesture, carelessly offered, has been received as a slight, rebuke or worse.

Ignatius gives valuable advice to Christians which applies equally well to friends and lovers of any faith or none. He recommends that we always seek to interpret a person's statements favourably while seeking to clarify any possible misinterpretations. If we find that the other is in error then still the best possible interpretation of the error will pave the way to correction and agreement. In other words give your partner the benefit of any doubt, clear up the doubt and be as charitable as possible. This is applicable to actions as well as words. One wonders how many human conflicts might be avoided if more of us followed it.

I think Jesus probably wanted to ask his companions at least once a day: 'Do you know what I have done to you?' So often did they misunderstand his actions and words. After the feeding of the five thousand we are told the crowd were convinced that Jesus was the one they had been waiting for, the one who would deliver them from Rome. So they became excited and looked as though they would take Jesus by force and make him their king. With alacrity Jesus disappeared, taking himself off into the hills to pray. No doubt he prayed for strength to cope with the fixation of his people on their erroneous image of the Messiah.

Perhaps he did ask the disciples, on his return that day, if they at least had understood the meaning of his actions with the crowd. We are not told. Perhaps he asked the question often, but the one time that is recorded for us appears at John 13.1–5 and after one of the most emotionally charged and possibly confusing moments yet shared by the group.

It was before the festival of the Passover, and Jesus knew that the hour had come for him to pass from this world to the Father. He had always loved those who were his in the world, but now he showed how perfect his love was.

They were at supper, and the devil had already put it into the mind of Judas Iscariot son of Simon, to betray him. Jesus knew that the Father had put everything into his hands, and that he had come from God and was returning to God, and he got up from table, removed his outer garment and, taking a towel, wrapped it round his waist; he then poured water into

a basin and began to wash the disciples' feet and to
wipe them with the towel he was wearing.

Jesus washes the disciples' feet. To them it was an act of
complete abasement, a task properly performed by the
lowliest slave in the household of a host. For Jesus it was
a demonstration of deep love and gratitude. When done
by a slave, there was nothing intimate about this hospitable service. We would feel the same way about having
our hair cut in a salon. A service we are happy to allow
another to provide. But when Jesus disrobed and knelt
before each disciple, the fact of their friendship, his position as Teacher among them, their expectations of him,
infused the act with a new and shocking intimacy that
made their senses reel.

Interestingly, Jesus had recently been the recipient of a
similar intimacy from a woman in the town. She had
burst into an all-male supper and flung herself at Jesus'
feet, washing them with the tears that flowed freely down
her face, tenderly wiping them dry with the hair that
hung loose about her shoulders veiling her face. She
caressed them with skilled fingers and expensive ointment,
kissing them to her lips.

The love given and received in this most intimate of
gospel encounters was multi-dimensional. In the air was
eros, *agape*, *philia* and *epithymia*. This washing of feet
had been passionate, sexual and deeply spiritual for the
woman. I think it was the same for Jesus. He was the only
person in the room not expressing noisy offence. While
others no doubt called for her to be dragged out of the
house, Jesus refused even to rebuff her, refused to feign
outrage and thereby protect himself from the full meaning

and significance of her erotic approach to him. He understood. He knew what she had done to him. And he was not afraid to accept the gift of her passionate, erotic self.

It may be a little new for some to consider Jesus as a sexual person. We need time to get used to the idea. Perhaps it will help to recall that the Latin root of our word 'sex' is *secare* and it means to cut off or divide from. Jesus was a man. He was divided from the experience of being a woman. He was sexed just as we all are.

Here is how Ronald Rolheiser (1990) describes human sexuality:

> It is a dimension of our self-awareness. It is our eros, that irrepressible demand within us that we love and that energy within us that enables us to love. Through it we break out of the shells of our own egos and narcissism. Through it we seek contact, communication, wholeness, community and creativity. Through sexuality we are driven and drawn beyond ourselves.

The experience of having his feet washed, dried, anointed, massaged, kissed could be a sexual experience without it occurring to Jesus or the woman to follow up with the act of sex together. Lewis Smedes (1993) points out that:

> Actually, whenever a man and a woman relate to each other as persons there is a sexual dimension in the relationship. The more deeply personal it is, the more sexually involved the relationship becomes. This does not mean that all personal encounters between a man and a woman are springboards to an embrace. But it does mean that there is present an undercurrent of varied and unpredictable sexual dynamics that we can

call psychic sexuality. It adds an indefinable tinge of adventure and excitement, uncertainty and curiosity to the relationship ... This we owe to our creation as male and female, not to some lecherous trait inherited from the Fall of man ... The more we affirm it with thanks the less likely we are to be deluded by the fear that any sexually exciting relationship will lead to the bedroom.

We have no record of Jesus being anything but celibate. But celibates are sexual people too. Those with the charism do not fear and denigrate the sexual dimension of an encounter. Rather they celebrate and respect it. They know that for celibates and non-celibates alike sexuality is far more than genital, and leads to the bedroom by choice rather than uncontrollable compulsion. As a grace celibacy is a particular expression of sexuality; a restraining from full consummation with one individual in order to experience a depth of intimacy with all people.

I think Jesus had this self-awareness; this sexuality in spades. Embracing his own *eros* was celibacy for him – a celibacy that shows us how to break out of those shells of ego and narcissism. Jesus is the one who demonstrates with his life the irrepressible demand of love. Love that draws us out of ourselves to seek contact with others. If being sexed means being divided from, then it also means being impelled to search for completion.

It was sexuality, his *eros*, that drove Jesus from the carpenter's shop in Nazareth to the bank of the river Jordan and to his own baptism into union with the Father. It was *eros* that impelled him towards Jerusalem and the completion of all of creation through union with it on the cross – an *eros* that irrepressibly demanded that he love and that gave him the inner energy to enable that love. And not just of one other. Jesus did not, I think, love only one woman or one man. He loved his companions but not just these. His celibacy was part of the love, the perfect love, he had for all of humanity.

This sexual man, Jesus, keenly aware of his own and of the woman's *eros*, felt privileged to experience her loving ministrations. Touch is such a powerful communication. Have you ever enjoyed a massage performed by a really skilled person? It is such a moving experience. One that communicates worth to the person being massaged. Even if I have paid for the service, still there is a recognition that these hands are unhurried and are taking great care. They seem to know just what I need, where my tension lies, how to relieve that tension. They are loving hands and unafraid. Unafraid, that is, to be part of someone's body in contact with mine. They tell me as they work that I am precious and deserve care, that I am alive and have a right to be so, that I am both spiritual and sexual in nature, and that both of these are good. The woman who washed Jesus' feet with her tears conveyed all of this to him. She wanted nothing from him; only to give her love. To express the depth of it, just once, before returning to her home, perhaps never to see him again. All this Jesus understood and gratefully accepted. No wonder she is to be remembered throughout history. What a gift she gave him!

And now, in the upper room on the night before his beloved companions would betray and desert him and with this profound physical, emotional, spiritual and sexual experience still fresh in his own memory, Jesus looked round the room at his companions. One of the saddest parts of bereavement is regret. Many people are tormented by regrets after the death of a loved one. They wish they had spent more quality time with the other, or that they had told the person just how significant their love had been.

Jesus had spent three years travelling around the villages of Palestine with his companions, and now he wanted to tell them, before it was too late, just how important their friendship, their company, had been to him. He wanted to follow the unknown woman's example and express his feelings for them in action. I imagine Jesus looking round the upper room. For me it looks like the top floor in a Scottish tenement building, because that is the kind of 'upper room' I know well. For you it might look quite different from this and from the typical Palestinian dwelling it undoubtedly was.

The companions had agreed to eat supper together that evening so I imagine smells of cooking meat and herbs, of strong wine and fresh bread. I can see the dancing shadows made on the walls and roof by the candles and can hear the buzz of conversations, the noises of eating and drinking, of shifting bodies on a wooden floor, of arms rubbing together momentarily as hands stretch out across the table for more food. And if I stay still long enough with this scene I begin to notice other things not directly connected to my five senses. I become aware of atmosphere, unspoken thoughts, emotions, tension, uncertainty, even fear.

As Jesus looks round he notices all of these things too. His face is half-illuminated by a nearby candle as his eyes gaze briefly on each man and woman there before coming to rest on a chair in the corner of the room. The chair is stacked full, in my imagination, with a luxurious pile of fresh, fragrant white towels. I know and now savour what these look like, feel like, smell like to me.

The sight of the towels reminds Jesus of the customary service that has been overlooked. He recalls his recent encounter in Simon's house. How it was overlooked there too. He recalled the woman and how good it felt to surrender to the knowing massage of her loving hands. He had felt so cared for at that moment. It's then that Jesus has his idea, because the towels are so inviting. I imagine he smiles as he rises from the table and picks one up, feeling the generous pile in his calloused fingers. He feels the way I do when I find just the right gift for someone I care for deeply. The room has fallen silent now and all eyes are watching in a disbelief that is giving way to embarrassment, even shame.

Peter's reaction is well known, as is the response Jesus makes to it. But now I try to imagine my own reaction, my own thoughts as this man kneels at my feet, undoes my sandals and carefully, gently, washes then dries each foot. I look down on his head, feel his hands on me, listen to his breathing and notice that my own breath is held, smell his fragrance, taste the dryness of my mouth.

Then he asks the question: 'Do you understand what I have done to you?' (John 13.12). No, they do not know. He has washed their feet and has thrown them into a confusion of questions. What has Jesus done to *himself* in this act? Has he humbled himself to the position of a household slave in carrying out this meanest of tasks? Or has he raised the household slave to a new position of respect, by taking this role? The disciples were all present when the woman wept and anointed his feet. They had been shocked and confused then too; the blatant sexual intimacy of the encounter had both repulsed and fascinated them. Now it seemed that Jesus was re-enacting her indiscretion with each of them. This was no longer the impersonal service of an anonymous slave. Their hearts were thudding loudly and tears were very close. This washing of feet was a disturbing experience, and its meaning was, for the present at least, lost in the storm of their emotions.

The truth is, Jesus intended to express his perfect love for them. He had sought contact, communication, wholeness, community and creativity in the three years they had been his companions, and in this act of washing feet he was seeking it still. This was a sexual act; it came from Jesus' self-awareness. It was an act of *eros* and *agape*. In taking the role of a slave Jesus demonstrated both the transforming power of self-giving love and the only true way to break out of the shells of our own egos and narcissism. He showed that contact, communication, wholeness, community and creativity become possible when we do. The disciples were now, as ever, driven and drawn beyond themselves by this most disturbing encounter with intimacy as powerful and tender as any they had known.

Jesus hopes they understand something of his passionate love and respect for each one of them. His hopes are not just for this latest and last encounter. He wonders if they know yet what the three years of intimate companionship with him has done to them. They have eaten together tonight, but they have eaten together many times before; eaten and slept and walked and talked and worked together. Do they realize that the whole experience of intimacy with him and with each other has affected them? Do they understand in what ways this has happened?

So too, when Jesus addresses the question to you and me: 'Do you know what I have done to you?' It is a question which invites us to reflect on the whole story of our lives. Do you know, do you understand what Jesus has done to you, since the day you were conceived, through all the years of your life, until this moment in time? He has poured graces over your tired feet. He has tenderly massaged them with love and honour; gently dried them with solicitous care; a towel wrapped round his waist. Do you know, can you glimpse the intensity of feeling he has for you, has held for you every day of your life? Can you feel the message communicated by the touch of Jesus? You are precious and deserve care. You are alive and have a right to be so. You are both spiritual and sexual in nature, and both of these are good.

It is an important question, one to contemplate at leisure. Answering it can let flow a river of gratitude within, which is capable of washing away many stains and soothing many hurts received along the way. Jesus longs to be understood by his companions, and you are one of them. There is something profoundly intimate about Christ's enquiry and we need to hear and answer it often if the grace of intimacy with him is to be ours. It is also an invaluable question for our personal relationships. Imagine asking it of your partner just after a long kiss. Does this other recognize the love that has been poured into them from your lips? Does he or she receive and understand your communication of deep desire, honour, strength and compassion?

Perhaps you might spend some time imagining that you are the one who, loving your own partner passionately, wants to express this love by washing or massaging the other's feet. Remind yourself of that earlier story by reading it in Luke 7.36. Don't concern yourself about what kind of woman this was. Luke tells us she had a bad name in town, but then if she didn't have one before this incident she had one after it. And remember Luke is writing his Gospel many years after. She was a woman, no better or worse than any other. A woman in love. Let that be enough.

Set the scene, but be kind to yourself. The woman in the story took her life in her hands by entering Simon's house and performing her act of love under the hostile gaze of at least 20 men. But you don't have to imagine yourself being so public. Choose safety and privacy in your imagination and compose the place with your senses.

Now be creative with your love. Play with all of your senses. Use fragrances, oils, massage, and imagine that these two feet are the only part of your partner's body that have any awareness. The only way he or she can know your love is through them. Do not shrink from the *eros* within you. Perhaps you will want to use your mouth and tongue to convey the meaning and depth of some emotion you feel for these feet. That is okay, isn't it? This is, after all *your* imagination and *your* partner.

When you are ready, again in your imagination, sit back on your heels and look into your partner's eyes and ask the question: 'Do you know and understand what I have done to you?' Let the responses come. Notice them, even the hilarious ones. Then take a little time to write in your journal whatever of this imaginative contemplation that you do not wish to lose or forget.

If you have enjoyed contemplating the washing or massaging of your partner's feet then of course you might want to try it for real, providing your partner acquiesces. Have fun and don't forget to ask the question. By doing so you will invite reflection, check out understanding and clear up any misunderstandings. You will also open the door to a lively sharing of encounter and experience. Encounter and experience are the soil from which intimacy may grow. Ignatius reflected that no amount of knowledge about God or the world can bring salvation but rather the deep experiential understanding of a very few simple truths.

To facilitate the experiential understanding of God Ignatius encourages a lengthy contemplation of Jesus as he journeys around the villages with his companions, teaching, healing, laughing together, playing with children, dancing at weddings. The grace that Ignatius recommends the exercitant to ask for in prayer is a deepening intimacy with Jesus. From his own experience Ignatius was confident that anyone who came to the contemplation of Jesus with an open and generous heart could not help but feel an attraction to this man. With a growing intimate knowledge the contemplative would surely fall in love with Jesus and finding himself in love would desire to follow the Lord closely, patterning his life on that of the Lord.

His observation holds true not only for the life of Christian faith but can be surprisingly fruitful for the relationship we are developing with our partner. A deep understanding of some simple truths can enrich and even save a relationship. These truths are there for all of us to notice if we take the time. Unfortunately no one is encouraging us to slow down and gaze around ourselves with the kind of relaxed attentiveness that would facilitate this noticing. Simple truths are so easily overlooked in the mad rush we like to call life.

So now I take some time and prayerfully consider my partner. I imagine him/her standing before me and addressing Christ's words to me: 'Do you know what I have done to you?'

- ▲ What has having this man/woman as a companion done to me and for me?
- ▲ Where are the times when I have held my breath at a sudden glimpse of intense feeling for me?
- ▲ What are the qualities this person has brought to my daily life that have been gifts?
- ▲ When has this person touched me in a new and surprising way?

I recall to mind and write down as many memories that seem to be responses to the question, put by my partner: 'Do you know what I have done to you?'

I may notice that some answers to the question as put by Jesus resemble my responses when the question is put by my partner. This happens because one of the ways that Jesus has affected me is through this man, this woman. One of the ways Christ has sought contact, communication, wholeness, community and creativity with me is through this love we share. This partnership has invited me, as Christ does, to break out of the shells of my own ego and narcissism. It has driven and drawn me beyond myself.

It may be time to revisit the earlier reflection we made on Christ's presence in the bedroom. Imagine him asking 'Do you know what I have done to you as you have made love to this other? Do you know what I hoped for you, desired for you, felt for you in each encounter?' Notice and note down any responses that present themselves to you. Then before we go on to our next contemplation give thanks for what Jesus has done to you through your daily living and loving with your partner.

References

Fromm, Erich, *The Art of Loving*. London, Harper Collins, 1995.

Rolheiser, Ronald, *Forgotten Among the Lillies*. London, Spire, 1990.

Smedes, Lewis, *Sex For Christians*. London, Triangle, 1993.

6

Unless You Become Like Little Children

All rich, intimate relationships are playful.

It is not simply that we all need a good giggle now and then or a fun night out, or to be reminded just how hilarious sex can be, though we do need all of these things. The fundamental approach to life, love and faith is meant to be a playful one. This is how it was in the beginning.

Have you ever tried to imagine creation from the perspective of the Father, Son and Holy Spirit? What was it the three persons of the Trinity experienced in creating life? Here is how Jürgen Moltmann sees it in his book *God In Creation* (1989). 'This creative God plays with his potentialities and creates out of nothing what is his good pleasure, because it corresponds to himself.' Can you sense the joyful intimacy of this playful creating? Can you imagine God playfully creating *you* out of an overabundance of potentialities corresponding to the Divine?

Try reading the creation accounts aloud in a playful voice. Perhaps you might rewrite the story of creation as a script with the Father, Son and Holy Spirit discussing various possibilities and chuckling together over the thought of the duck-billed platypus. Try to list the potentialities of God that have been sown into your being. Do not limit yourself to the gifts, qualities, talents that you are aware of having but also those you would like to have. This will give you a far more accurate picture of the person God is in the process of creating. You will discover that the creation of our world, of you, is as effortless as the imaginary play of a five-year-old.

Sadly we have forgotten the grace of effortless play that is the image of God in us. Adults are children with amnesia. We have forgotten that play is intrinsic to the grace of intimacy and therefore to our salvation. Forgotten too that life is a miracle and everything in it a gift entirely for us.

It is time to remember. Remember that unity is our first experience. Mother and child are one. There is no separation. Play is the earliest exploration of self and world. A discovery of where 'I' end and the rest begins. A baby's play consists mostly of mouthing things. By experiencing an object with my mouth I know it and discover the boundaries between it and me. Each discovery is a gift.

I encounter interesting others and soon develop peek-a-boo games. I practise smiles that are reflections of their smiling faces and quickly learn the subtle differences between the smiling 'ah' of delight and the sympathetic 'ah' of concern. By four months I have discovered that I can use my hands to make something happen; hitting a rattle with a tiny fist will make a sound. It is a delightful and intoxicating discovery; a miracle. A few months on and mobility is the goal. The horizons of an already exciting world widen to welcome an intrepid explorer as she scuttles into every new corner and cupboard. By the age of four I have added sociability to my playing skills and creative imagination is now my favoured toy. I am an artist, a musician, an actor, an explorer, a scientist, a storyteller and poet, a magician. A child of genius.

A child at play is a creative and imaginative being with a task in life, a mark to make. In play he explores and develops his desire to understand what moves creation, self and others and the particular role he has in the universe. God is well pleased.

By the age of seven every child is a gifted and unconscious teacher of play. Their effortless expertise is beautifully captured by Andrew Greeley (1984):

> The child does not need a definition of play, and no one has to teach him how to be playful. Play is a world unto itself, a game with its own rules, its own parameters, its own constraints. It is real, indeed, terribly real; but it is quite distinct from the mundane world of everyday events. The child does not confuse the game with the rest of life. The boundary lines are firm, but within those boundaries the rules of the game replace the rules of the real world. His game is competitive, imaginative, festive, fantastic; it is intricate, subtle, involved. It is played only with friends, with those you trust, with those you care about. Strangers are not welcome into the game – not until they stop being strangers. The game is spontaneous, but it is also disciplined. Any spontaneity that breaks the rules of the game will destroy it. The game is fun, but it is also serious; it is competitive, but the rules must be strictly observed.

I think this is what Jesus observed watching some children at play together in the late afternoon sun. Imagine the scene as though you were Jesus.

You perhaps spent the morning teaching a crowd about the Kingdom of God. As always there were voices of ridicule and malice. The ceaseless efforts of a few to trick you into blasphemy in addition to the desperate cries for help from the sick and the poor have left your head buzzing. Gratefully you rest beneath a tree in this village square and watch some children at play.

They do not notice you watching, so involved in their own world are they. You know this game, played it with your pals when you were this age. And you have no desire to break the spell with comment or applause. An enthusiastic spectator, you silently cheer on first one child then another. There is fierce competition and imaginative interpretation of the game. There is laughter and agonized groans, thrills and disappointments. Sometimes an argument breaks out when one child has forgotten or mischievously ignored a convention or rule of the game. Noisily the child is rounded on and told to play fairly or not at all. Usually the culprit is content to fall in line once more and the dispute is quickly forgotten.

The sun begins to set, the light to disappear. Mothers begin to drift out of doorways followed by inviting smells of cooking and an assortment of infants. The game must end and the children protest loudly until the smell of supper reaches their nostrils and suddenly they become aware of their empty stomachs. Meanwhile the mothers have spotted you sitting now with eyes closed, head resting on a tree, half aware of the sounds around you, half dreaming of other summer afternoons and other children playing. And beyond these memories of childhood another dream of play and of union and perfect intimacy dances on the fringes of your consciousness. There is within you a knowing that only comes from experience, a recognition that playful intimacy is at the heart of your existence. You sense a coming home to a truth more familiar than your own name and gratitude fills your heart until it feels it must overflow or burst. The setting sun makes one last valiant effort to blaze before giving way to dusk and for one brief moment these breathless children are incandescent in its light, their laughter pealing out and touching heaven itself. And touching your heart also.

Meanwhile, recognizing you, some mothers catch hold of children's hands and bring them to you for a blessing:

> When the disciples saw this they turned them away. But Jesus called the children to him and said, 'Let the little children come to me, and do not stop them; for it is to such as these that the kingdom of God belongs. I tell you solemnly, anyone who does not welcome the kingdom like a little child will never enter it.' (Luke 18.15–17)

As you speak, the words sing out their truth within your spirit. This is the Good News – that the Kingdom of God belongs in the heart of a child. Passionate and playful union is the secret of eternal life.

This passage is pivotal to the Gospel. Jesus' solemn declaration that the Kingdom belongs to children is on a par with his claim to be one with the Father. Both claims were so outrageous as to render them unforgettable during that long period of oral tradition before the Gospels were committed to paper. Unfortunately the startling revelation about the Kingdom recorded in Luke 18 makes little impact on modern ears. We think we know what the text is saying, forgetting that familiarity with a text is different from an intimate knowledge and appreciation of it.

Jesus emphatically proclaimed the importance of children in an age when childhood was short and often brutal. Not much has changed in 2000 years. Children today are made homeless, they live in sewers, they are kidnapped and coerced into children's armies, made sex-slaves at the age of nine, have limbs summarily amputated by machete-wielding strangers or are blown up by landmines planted in their playground. In the more developed countries they are faced with drugs, drink, paedophiles, along with the dangers of consumerism, fashion, broken homes, and the universal fact of hidden domestic violence. Childhood is still short and unspeakably brutal.

'It is to such as these that the kingdom of God belongs.' Jesus is not saying we don't need to concern ourselves unduly about the horrors society inflicts on its own children because all their suffering will be made up for in a heaven-later-on. He is saying that the Kingdom of Heaven is like a game played by children. It is a world other than the daily world of careworn adults, a space quite unlike any other. A place of confidence and courage and vulnerability and laughter and competitiveness and compassion and simple joy. It is close by and accessible to all. And it is a gift.

'The Kingdom of God is very near to you' (Luke 10.9). Not near as an approaching train is near to a station and expected soon to arrive. Jesus did not want people to live as though waiting for the arrival of a new dispensation that would steam into their lives and rescue them from all suffering and hardship. Jesus wanted his listeners to recognize that the Kingdom of God was already as near to them as it ever would be. It is up close, all around, within and without each person. The Kingdom of God is very near, very intimate. Indeed there can be nothing more intimate, for the Kingdom is God at play with creation, with us. A simple enough truth that any of us might understand.

Young children do not know the laws of the land, the intricacies of the judicial system. Yet Charles Dickens said of them: 'In the little world in which children have their existence . . . there is nothing so finely perceived and so finely felt as injustice.' I think the same is true about their knowledge of the Kingdom. Children have a finely perceived and finely felt experiential knowledge of God's loving intention for creation.

Sometimes adults remember this knowledge too, and often it is in the act of sex. Good sex is passionate union with another and at least potentially with the Kingdom. Sometimes the Kingdom within us is remembered as all the fragments of memory and desire and experience come together in an explosive blaze of something very like glory. For a brief ecstatic moment our consciousness is altered and we glimpse the miracle of life: we are not alone, either in the bed or in the universe.

Sex is one way forgetful adults can enter the Kingdom of God like little children. When an encounter beneath the sheets is playful – competitive, imaginative, festive, fantastic, spontaneous – the Kingdom is very near. It is a game of Chase and Catch accompanied by much giggling, teasing, role-playing and fierce competition. Everything is at stake for the duration of the game but nothing is really at stake. The two players will live to play together another day. And so it is with the Kingdom: God at intimate play with creation.

Of course there is an alternative to intimacy, to play and to the Kingdom of God, as Andrew Greeley (1984) points out: 'Sex is either playful or it becomes a difficult burden, an obligation, a tension release that produces only minimal satisfaction.' There is oppressive proximity. An intimate relationship is either playful or it is oppressive and often dangerously so. Sadly such oppressive proximity is common to both religion and relationships.

Let us first turn our attention to oppression as it manifests itself in religion. An oppressive faith manifests itself as a difficult burden to the believer and an obligation. The person feels guilty about the quality of their relationship to the God of their faith and only ever experiences temporary release of this guilt through the practice of religious worship and service. Fear is present and goads the person into making unasked-for sacrifices of themselves, their family or of the stranger in their community. God is not intimate, just too close for comfort. Psalm 139 is not a reassurance but a threat:

> You know if I am standing or sitting,
> you read my thoughts from far away,
> whether I walk or lie down, you are watching,
> you know every detail of my conduct.

Unfortunately this oppressive faith in God is often the only one being shared between one believer and another: father to son, mother to daughter, neighbour to neighbour. Until quite recently the only alternatives to this oppressive faith lay in atheism, humanism or agnosticism. The recent New Age spirituality is most charitably understood as a fourth alternative: a variety of attempts to garner a faith in the beauty and mystery of the world from the evidence of nature and from our own sense of the spiritual dimension of life. I think Jesus might rejoice in this attempt to leave behind the worst excesses of oppressive world faiths. He might say to a New Age enthusiast: 'You are not far from the Kingdom of God' (Mark 12.34). However, at least one step more needs to be taken by the most authentic seeker in the New Age philosophy, as we shall see.

How near are you to the Kingdom? How can you gauge your own relationship of faith and discover if it is passionate union, an oppressive proximity, or a well-intentioned search for personal development? Reading over Psalm 139 might provide a clue. Read it aloud but in a quiet, intimate voice; God is closer to you than you are to yourself so there is no need to project your voice. Notice how you feel about a God who reads your thoughts and knows (and presumably understands) every detail of your conduct. Are you amazed at how wonderfully and fearfully you are made? Or are you inclined, like the Psalmist, to escape such intimacy?

I often speak to people who sense there must be something *more* to the life of faith than their present experience. They are seeking a deeper intimacy with God, but they, like the Psalmist, also have fears. They are afraid that to come closer to God will be to court disaster. Some part of them insists that playing with God is dangerous. That one can expect to lose and lose badly. These people believe that intimacy with God carries a huge price-tag; that God

102

requires costly sacrifice from those who seek him, that nothing in life is gift. For most people the sacrifice they imagine is unbearably personal: an illness, a bereavement, loss of a job, failure of a relationship, a child in danger – these are some of the entrance fees to the Kingdom of God.

God is not the one requiring sacrifice, we are. While healthy, secure children start each new game afresh with all infringements cancelled and all arguments forgotten, religious grown-ups store up not only each hurt felt but each perceived failing of their own. We cannot play with God this day because yesterday or 20 years ago we played unfairly or made an error of judgement, and we believe God is like us and remembers every detail.

My husband has a memory from childhood. A much younger boy who lived in the same street of tenements would come to the door and ask of the adult who opened it to him: 'Is Jackie coming out to play?' Now his parents understood that Jackie did not want to play with this infant so they, hoping not to cause hurt, would convey the message that Jackie was busy doing homework. Undaunted the little chap at the door would lisp hopefully through wobbly baby teeth: 'Is he coming out tomorrow?'

God only wants us to come and play. We find such persistence charming in an infant but embarrassingly gauche in our God. We prefer to cope with the belief that God requires us to be fearful and nervous of him, ready to pay for our mistakes and our sins. This belief, however, is insupportable by any contemplation of the life and teaching of Jesus. If you read the Gospels it is hard to avoid the conclusion that sins, our wicked acts of commission and omission, were not a big problem for Jesus.

He forgave them in the Father's name, and it was a simple thing. 'Courage, my son! Your sins are forgiven' (Matthew 9.2); 'Your sins are forgiven . . . Your faith has saved you; go in peace' (Luke 7.48–50). Now let us get on with this exciting game called life.

Jesus seems to have felt no need to distance himself from sinful folk, no need to advocate elaborate ceremonies and purges before enjoying fellowship with them. The religious leaders, these children with amnesia, found it extremely hard to accept that freedom from sin and guilt could be so simple and so final. The whole Temple system of animal sacrifices had been developed and was now perpetuated by the constant necessity of ordinary people to atone for the latest breaking of the covenant grace which bound them to God and made them righteous. Whenever this covenant relationship with God was broken through disobedience, ignorance or mere accident the remedy was the same. The transgressor procured an unblemished animal and laid upon it the task of mending the broken relationship through the shedding of its blood.

When you think about it the sacrificial system is an elaborate version of the child's game of tag. If you are caught you must stand still until someone frees you by tapping you on the shoulder. Then you can rejoin the game. Similarly when one infringed a cultic law one's religious and often community life was put on hold until the sacrificial lamb or bird set one free again to rejoin both community and cult.

Given their tried and tested system for atonement, the religious leaders of the time could not help but be offended at one who forgave breaches of the covenant so casually, and in God's name no less! It was probably the

most provocative utterance of Jesus: 'Your sins are forgiven.' Like something a child might say as he playfully
tapped a friend's shoulder and set him free to rejoin the
game of tag.

Indeed we are told that they were hard pressed to
decide which shocked them more: the healing of a para-
lysed man or the forgiveness of that man's sins. You can
see their point. After all, the Temple had served its purpose for centuries safeguarding communication between
man and God and God and man. Now this upstart from
Nazareth seemed to be suggesting that the Temple system
of sacrifices was a misunderstanding, and animal sacrifice
unnecessary since God would never cut himself off from
intimate communication with creation. This thought
was just too radical to be entertained, and not only by the
religious leaders of Jesus' acquaintance.

For us it begs the question about the cross. If Christ
could forgive sins so simply, and if God did not need a
go-between of even a dove, let alone the Lamb of God,
what was the cross about? For the New Age enthusiasts
the question of the cross is an irrelevance of course but to
the Christian it is central to intimacy. It is the one thing
necessary and we will contemplate it closely in chapter 8.

For now, let a child teach us. Here is a story that most
of us need to hear at least once a day. It concerns a priest
in a remote village and a child who it seems is in direct
contact with God. The priest hears stories around the
village and is concerned so he summons the child to him
and asks her: 'Is it true that God speaks to you in your
prayers?' The child answers, 'Yes, sir.' The priest seriously
doubts the child's experience but knows how to test her.
He suggests that next time God is speaking to her she ask

the Divine to tell her what the priest's secret sin is. He was pretty confident that, since he had never confessed this sin to another living soul, the child could have no way of knowing what it was.

Some weeks passed until the child appeared before the priest. He looked at her and asked: 'Has God been speaking to you then?'

'Yes, sir.'

'And did you ask God what my sin was?'

'Yes, sir.'

'And what did God reply?'

'God said, "I cannot remember."'

Then the priest knew that the child and God were indeed intimate friends.

God cannot remember and is not using any Divine creativity to recall the sins of the world. It is we who cannot forget them. When we become like little children we let ourselves off the hook, allow a new day to dawn, a new game to begin. We welcome all comers and the Kingdom of God is alive and active among us.

Now let us consider how oppressive proximity is manifest in a personal relationship. Imagine the scene. Conversation is monosyllabic and often snappish. It covers only the necessities of life: who will take the car for its MOT, when the plumber will arrive to fix the heating, how soon the annual holiday to Spain should be booked. Recreational pastimes are pursued individually: he golfs, she plays bridge once a week with some girl friends. Sex is on Saturday nights and she dreads it from the moment her eyes open in the morning. Her body refuses to respond to this man's hands. The changing rhythms of his breathing tell her what stage they are at in foreplay and are as predictable as the number of socks he puts in the laundry basket every week. There is no violence in this marriage, no obvious or intended abuse, simply a sense of obligation that feels like a stranglehold around her throat. The only danger she faces is this slow death of her passionate self dragged out for another 20 years.

The man too feels less than playful about his marriage and wonders where it all went wrong. The woman he married was intelligent, warm and very attractive. Her body was an endless source of fascination to him and sex was good. Perhaps she was a little fastidious but he had accommodated this peccadillo. Foot odour, he had quickly learned, was the ultimate abomination so he had quickly developed a routine of showering every morning and again in the evening before dinner, changing his socks each time. And so they had settled down to married life reasonably amicably and the years rolled along. Work, children, money worries had all taken a toll on their relationship but he had assumed that was normal and even necessary. Now however it seems to the man that he and his wife share a lifestyle rather than a relationship. Though his wife continues to be really attractive her own uninterest in her body and his has eroded his confidence and eventually his enthusiasm. He is weary of trying and in danger of slipping from maturity into old age long before the years ask this of him.

In your imagination look around your acquaintances. How many seem to manifest something of this oppressive proximity? How many broken marriages around you are desperate flights from it? What about your own relationship? Where is intimacy and where is oppressive proximity in it?

Familiarity, shared goals, common interests, joint labour and child-raising: most marriages have some or all of these good elements yet none of them can produce the intimacy for which we long. Taken as a whole and without large dollops of play they have at least the potential to sabotage it. If it is not to degenerate into an insufferable proximity intimacy must be playful. Two people living closely together and coping with all the pressures and responsibilities and uncertainties of modern life need to remember how to play imaginatively together. Then they will become once more artists, musicians, actors, explorers, scientists, storytellers, poets and magicians.

Of course, remembering how to play is a grace. Imagine Jesus once more at the village square. The game is 'Chase and Catch'. Try to put yourself in Jesus' skin. What is it that delights him as he watches the game? What makes him laugh, gasp, tense in delighted excitement? What is it about these children, this game, that feels so right to him and a reminder of not only his own childhood but of his pre-existence with Father and Spirit?

Now imagine that Jesus watches you and your partner at play. If the playfulness of your relationship has been buried beneath a decade or two of responsibility then you may have to cast your mind back quite far to find a useful memory. The same point applies here as for any good memory. Do not look for a huge episode. Be content with a small memory of playfulness; a brief encounter. Recollect what was most delightful about it. Look for signs of intimacy: play that is competitive, imaginative, festive, fantastic and intricate, subtle, involved. Look for spontaneity but do not overlook discipline. Intimacy is fun but it is also serious; it is competitive, but some rules are necessary and need to be observed. The most playful lovers know these things and respect the rules and constraints while continually developing their skills and discovering new subtleties of the game.

Notice too your own reactions as you allow the memory to affect you in the here and now. If play is not a lively part of your present experience you may notice a feeling of sadness, of something lost and missed. Be hospitable to all your feelings. This sadness too is a grace. When a relationship runs out of wine I think very often it is because two people have forgotten how to play. Patient and honest prayer, talking to Jesus about the situation as we did in chapter 4, will lead you grace by grace to the Kingdom of intimate play. You will rediscover that intimacy is a game of 'Chase and Catch' where lovers seek, hide, flee, pursue, tease and laugh in the delicious pleasure of it all. And the Kingdom of God is among us.

References

Greeley, Andrew M., *Love and Play*. London, W. H. Allen, 1984.
Moltmann, Jürgen, *God In Creation*. London, SCM Press, 1985.

7

What Do You Want?

Intimacy involves disclosure.

When I am intimate with you I give you deep knowledge of and influence over me. You of course reciprocate or the intimacy is destroyed. Intimacy requires both of us to communicate knowledge of ourselves to the other. One way to encourage such communication is by asking often the question 'What do you want me to do for you?' (Matthew 20.33). It is an invitation to disclosure.

Answering, I reveal something of my self, my personality, my present mood, my desires, and if I am confident enough in our relationship even my sexual fantasies. The question also invites me to exert my influence over you. Intimacy requires that you at least attempt to meet my request, answer my longings, play with me. This is true whether you are my partner or my God.

When we try to disclose our desires to another or The Other we may encounter two difficulties. We do not know what it is that we really want and we are unsure of what we can have. Knowing what we want is difficult because we have so many desires within us at any one time and we lack practice in the art of discerning them.

What Do You Want?

A young mother of pre-school children might desire sleep, fun, a pampering makeover, someone to tackle the housework, abandoned sex, a grown-up conversation. All these desires are present at the one time. When her husband asks what he can do for her she is plunged into a sea of these and other desires: she wants her own identity back, her career, her colleagues, the creative power unleashed by her profession. She longs to burn her nursing bra and return to more frivolous underwear. She longs to seduce her lover with confidence and power. But also she wants to be the best mother ever, she longs to help her children discover the wonders of the world and of the bottom of their garden. She wants to be wise and calm and funny and reassuring for them. This brief plunge into her surface desires may well exhaust her last ounce of energy. She will settle for an hour's sleep.

Our souls are oceans of desire. They have many seas, tides, currents, depths and shorelines. An ocean can be dangerously stormy one minute and all tranquillity the next. What is happening on the surface rarely reflects what is happening just below the surface. The ocean floor is another world altogether.

Ignatius believed that we can find God in everything of our lived experience. Our desires are part of that lived experience and an excellent starting point on our quest for intimacy with God. That is why Ignatius advised that each time we go to prayer we begin by asking God for what it is we want and desire. He encourages each of us to become an expert diver in our own ocean, able to find and bring to the surface many valuable pearls.

My desires are many and varied, and each one has its own importance. Some of them are passing, others are significant signposts for my life. Some offer peace, justice and liberation but not all of them do. Desires are risky, but they are the soul of my faith, and like Mary: 'My soul proclaims the greatness of the Lord'. They will lead me to intimate union with God if only I can trust that God is in my desire. Actually none of my desires are perfectly pure and healthy; they are never that simple, nor do I have to make them so.

For example, I desire to involve myself in the worshipping community of my local church. Does this mean I desire God? Well no. I may want to attend because the people there are warm, loving, and it feels good to be near them. I may involve myself in some activity or service because it gives me a sense of satisfaction or worth, even of power. I may pray regularly because being seen as a praying person carries some kudos. I may want God but my wanting is only a vague restlessness: a sense that something lies beyond my present experience of life in the community of faith.

It is okay to accept with appropriate sorrow that my desires are shot through with conceit, deceit and selfishness. It is okay because in spite of all this they are fired by God's gracious desire for intimacy with me. Ignatius discovered that God is not afraid or put off by our ambivalence, our hidden agendas, our lustful desires for wealth, honour and power. I may desire all three but behind these lies something I really desire, and behind that something I really, really desire. Behind all my desires is God, desiring me. So God and I reach for one another, through the ocean of my soul. God knows that our true destiny, the great pearl, is intimacy. That we must dive deep to find it.

So if I do not know what I really want, I can discover this by attending to all the desires I sense swimming around within me. Sensing, however, may take some practice. Let me explain.

Awareness of both the world outside of my body, and my own inner world, is possible, because I have sense organs, capable of receiving messages, in the form of stimuli. These messages are carried to the brain, where they are interpreted to form images of the world. This process of receiving, translating and transmitting messages from the outside world to the brain is called sensation. The interpretation by the brain of the messages received is called perception. Exploring my desires is only possible if I am aware of sensation and able to interpret what I sense.

During the years of childhood I received stimuli continuously from parents, teachers, peer-group, advertisers, media, government, church, society, culture. All of these messages were interpreted by me to form images of reality and truth. As a child I learned what I lived. Childhood may have been good, bad or indifferent. Whichever it was, it matters less than the sad fact that many adults are still living what they learned in childhood, even though the stimuli they are now receiving could be interpreted differently, if only the brain was engaged in the process. Being open to sensation allows new ideas, deeper truths, a wider vision to be glimpsed. It is one important way of becoming like children so that we can enter the Kingdom. But I am lazy. Instead of perceiving anew, I save some energy by habitually relying upon old perceptions. Instead of being an explorer my brain is a clerk sorting efficiently through my filing cabinet of perceptions to find the best fit for my present experience.

I have noticed that those who talk to me about their prayer rarely use the word 'sense', but often tell me what they 'think' is going on. Often their thoughts are perceptions that have been filed away years ago and are now retrieved, dusted off and presented without any reference to the senses. So the person tells me what he thinks a Scripture passage means for life in the twenty-first century. Then I ask: 'What does your gut tell you?' By 'gut' I mean the bodily senses, all of them. Silence. Then slowly, tentatively, a deeper truth is liberated within the praying person. A startlingly different truth from anything yet perceived.

So a man thinks that God is often disappointed with him. This perception of reality has been filed away, probably since childhood. It may have been re-inforced on a weekly basis from the pulpit of his church and is one of the more dog-eared files in his cabinet, often trotted out to explain life. But if the man allows his senses to carry their current messages about God to his brain and if he can courageously interpret those messages without slavish reference to the earlier perception, he may discover that God has never been disappointed in him.

The contemplative approach to life and to prayer can strengthen our facility for sensing and perceiving. Practice takes time but quickly becomes enjoyable and enriching. It can be done alone or with a partner.

Go for a walk and become aware of your senses. Stop walking for a second each time some new stimulus is received. You hear a dog bark, pause. You smell the sea, pause. You taste the salt in your mouth, pause. You feel the wind on your face, pause. Soon you will pause because you sense a feeling within: joy, sorrow, excitement, anxiety, laughter, anger. Ask yourself: What is it that I want now?

With a partner try massage. One massages the other but both try to become aware of every sensation, describing each one, answering the unspoken questions: What do I see, what do I hear, what can I taste, smell, what am I touching and what is touching me? Again we may become aware of emotion and desire. 'What do you want me to do for you?' is the natural question to ask.

In contemplative prayer we take time to compose the place of a gospel story, asking ourselves: What do I see, hear, smell, taste, touch or feel? It is equally fruitful to ponder what Jesus senses and to ask him: 'What do you want me to do for you?' At the end of a time of contemplative prayer I often ask myself: What feelings or emotions am I aware of now? I am pretty sure that feelings, whatever they may be, are fine. I feel sad – that is fine. I feel angry – that too is fine. I feel euphoric – that is fine. I feel confused – that too is fine. My feelings are messages and each one can be made welcome whether it makes me feel comfortable or uncomfortable. Each one will help me perceive my true desires.

Asking myself what I want, and interpreting stimuli anew is risky of course because the feelings and desires I identify through interpreting my bodily senses will vary in strength and significance. The strong emotion that can accompany a desire may be alarming. Some feelings can mislead and many desires are born of self-worship and hedonism. In the face of these risks it may seem safer not to go diving at all.

So we tell ourselves that we want whatever the crowd endorses as acceptable and normal at this stage of life and faith. In a crowd of 20-year-olds we want uncomplicated sex without ties. When our peers are approaching 30 we want success, at 40 we want more success, at 50 we want security. In a religious crowd we want whatever the crowd believes God has in mind (rarely is this intimacy). But how many of us are content with life at 20, 30, 40, 50? Is it not evident that no matter how devoutly we stay in the crowd we still sense that there is more to life than this?

Which brings us to the second difficulty we encounter when we reflect on our desires. What am I allowed to ask for? What may I ask of my partner: in the routine of life, and most importantly in bed? What may I ask God for?

When things are hectic or trying or just mundane I will say half-jokingly to my husband: 'When are you going to take me away from all this?' Usually we are in the middle of a hastily snatched embrace as we meet briefly in a room of our noisy house; each intent on separate errands. I am sharing a small and quite fleeting fantasy of being whisked off to a new life or for a weekend in Paris, or even for a simple drive in the country. Which of these I have in mind is not stipulated. It does not need to be. This little exchange has been going on since our earliest days together and it is always a light-hearted but nevertheless intimate moment. My question is a response to the unspoken question of his embrace: 'What do you want me to do for you?'

I am like those disciples of John who followed Jesus and when asked by him 'What do you want?' (John 1.38) could only answer with another question. My response 'When are you taking me away from all this?' has an effect. I feel my husband's shoulders broaden at the suggestion that he has it within his power to whisk me off anywhere.

What Do You Want?

Our next encounter in bed is likely to be just as thrilling and surprising as any romantic weekend away could be.

Remember the wedding at Cana? I wonder if Jesus saw his mother approach with a request already in her eyes. Perhaps his own eyes made the enquiry even before she spoke: 'What do you want me to do for you?' I think her answer surprised him, was the last thing he expected.

Probably he anticipated a request for him to go and speak with old Aunt Sarah sat in the corner of the room looking wistfully at the dancers and remembering her dear departed husband. Jesus was surprised by his mother's request for a miracle and at first he was not inclined to oblige. But he loved his mother and respected her judgement. So he considered for a moment while she advised the servants to do whatever he told them. After this moment's reflection he was persuaded that solving the difficulty over the wine might be a good enough idea. He surrendered to her wishes.

From that day on Jesus seems to have asked the question often of those seeking his help. He was humbly and honestly interested in the person as an individual and did not assume that he knew their desires without being told. He did not insist on his own way in an arrogant belief about what was right for the other. Consequently when he visited his home town of Nazareth very few miracles happened there because very few people wanted them. What they mostly wanted in Nazareth was peace and quiet and this crowd of tourists flocking after the carpenter's son to move on to another village and stop blocking the roads and drinking from the well. To the unspoken question 'What do you want me to do for you?' the people of Nazareth would have replied: 'Go away.' Which is exactly what Jesus did.

117

I think Jesus is still asking the question simply, directly and without any hidden agenda: 'What do you want me to do for you?' We may answer with a question: What may we ask God for? None of us would feel abashed at requesting the kind of things most people identify with for a moderately happy existence – biological needs satisfied, safety, love and belongingness, a measure of self-esteem, and intellectual stimulation, even a hint of aesthetic appreciation.

These desires of ordinary, healthy individuals were identified by the psychologist Victor Maslow and he ordered them in a pyramid shape. The most basic needs of food and shelter he placed as the base of the pyramid. Only when these basic needs are met do we awaken to our desire for love, and so we begin to work through the pyramid layers.

At the pinnacle of Maslow's pyramid, above intellectual stimulation and aesthetic appreciation is self-actualization. I think Jesus would have understood this term to mean 'life in all its fullness', and of course Jesus declared that he came that we might have this life in all fullness. But notice that the top of a pyramid is an exposed and lonely position. My desire to discover and live the full meaning of my self may well be accompanied by a fear of exposure and of stepping beyond the normal and acceptable desires of the crowd. To further complicate matters I may have inherited a strong perception that self-actualization contradicts Christianity's teaching on self-denial. It seems reprehensible to pursue life in all fullness for my self.

Being a Scot, I have experience of being in the crowd of people who fear to risk the top of the pyramid. In Scotland we seem to feel animosity towards any who try to improve themselves, make a success of a business venture; anything which requires a breaking away from the crowd norms. When a person tries and fails, we show little sympathy, declaring, audibly or silently, that we knew it would all end in tears. Small wonder that so many Scots leave their homeland and can be found all over the world bringing innovations to every field of human endeavour.

Life with the crowd is safe. But then whoever promised that life would be safe? While the crowd form a sheltering community around me Christ calls me through my desires to the very pinnacle of possibilities for my unique life. What that pinnacle is matters not at all but desiring it with all my heart, mind, soul, is an authentic expression of love for the Lord God. It is obedience to the first commandment, a suitable response to the manifestation of the glory of God that is within each of us.

What may I ask of the Lord of all life? Nothing less than life in all its fullness. Sadly many devout people worship not the Lord of life in all fullness, but a god who demands sacrifice. A god who insists that they disregard their own desires, dreams, frailties even, in order to obey the divine will. Denial of self in big ways, or in many little ways is the only way to progress on the spiritual journey. I must lay down my life, rather than live it to the full.

One woman wrote in her journal of the God who can be depended upon to ask her to do the hard thing. The 'hard thing' of course can be almost comforting in its certainty and sameness to everything that has gone before. Since God always demands the hard thing I am at least familiar with this route of self-denial. And who knows, the struggle to sacrifice may become easier as my life wears on. Unfortunately this constant sacrificing does not stop at self. It becomes habit to offer up those in society I perceive to be different for sacrifice in my holocaust of fear. It is comforting to place the responsibility for all of society's ills on their shoulders. Is this really what God asks from men and women? Is God pleased when we scapegoat ourselves or others? When we are dominated by love rather than seduced by it? I think not.

I think God expects to have influence and power over those who know him and are known by her. But I believe we also have influence and power. By God's grace I am as capable of seducing God as God is of seducing me. Is this not what Mary the mother of Jesus discovered at Cana? Her intercession changed a small part of the destiny of the young couple, and even the destiny of Jesus, whose statement 'My hour has not come yet' (John 2.5) was surely changed as water turned to wine.

God is like a passionate lover and delights to be seduced by a loved one. To love someone is to give them this influence, this power over you. A relationship is all but over when one partner is unmoved by the wishes of the other. These two may share a home, a routine, even a bed but they have ceased to be one flesh. Bit by bit, decision by decision, they are going their separate ways.

So what may I ask of my partner? Anything that lies within the limits of possibility and a healthy respect for life and outwith coercion of body or conscience. I cannot say where exactly these limits will lie for you and your partner. I can only suggest that they probably lie somewhere beyond your present perceptions of them. 'Try it and see' is sound counsel.

When I disclose my desires to my partner I am confident that he will try his best to accommodate them, always supposing that I have not asked for the impossible.

And if my partner wants something from me that I am not immediately inclined to give then, because I love him, because this love gives him influence over me, I remain open to persuasion, education, even seduction to his request.

When we are playing together in safety we can risk the excitement and danger of such seduction. Since nothing is at stake we can allow the overcoming of our perceived boundaries of decency. We are free to disclose more and more about our inner life of emotions, desires, fantasies.

Where two people get together with no more involvement than genital excitement, they are really only masturbating in tandem. And they do not experience each other on the whole spectrum. But where sexual encounter is a total and unreserved experience of two persons, a mystery is present that no one can fathom. There is an unveiling of the self to another; but even when one has disrobed his selfhood to another, the mystery of his self is still deep, intriguing, and unexplored. Hence, the sexual probing of one another never ends; it must be repeated over and over again. This is one reason why sexual intercourse, the radical exposure, is so intriguing and electric – and yet incomplete. One has to come back again, not just because the hormones have been recharged and need release, but because so much always remains untapped in the human encounter.

(Smedes, 1993)

Of course some things might never be disclosed between even the most intimate of couples. However long we live together, however much we know about one another,

121

however deep our intimacy there will always be still *more* to this person than I can imagine or conceive.

That this is so ensures my endless captivity. It also means that whatever is disclosed is all the more significant and conducive to intimacy. So when I ask 'What would you like me to do for you?' I know that the answer is a gift of disclosure and of trust. Asking the question I avoid taking my partner for granted. Answering honestly and with imagination discloses who you are today and invites me to an encounter which may be surprising but will rarely disappoint. What dreams and desires do you have for your relationship? What do you want your partner to do for you?

Take a page in your journal and jot down whatever comes to mind. You may find it useful to reflect on the following areas:

⅄ Practicalities of Life
⅄ Emotional Life
⅄ Sex Life
⅄ Spiritual Life
⅄ Recreational Life

Try not to judge what you are writing. Do not censor your desires. Each one is significant so be hospitable to them all.

You may want to consider other areas of your life: career, family, faith. What are your desires for each? What do you want Jesus to do for you? What do you want your partner to do for you? Dream your dreams for life, faith, for your relationship with your partner and with God. This list may take a few days of prayer to feel complete. Take your time. See how honest and even outrageous you can allow yourself to be. When you feel that the list is a good snapshot of your dreams and desires at the moment sit with it in relaxed contemplation. Mark with highlight pen any item that moves you.

Ignatius believed that Christ calls us all to our deepest, truest self – that this is life in all its fullness. We become aware of Christ's call in many ways. A feeling of 'there must be more to life' stirs within us at work, at play, in our dreams and through poetry, art, music, sport, sex. Consequently anything on this list that makes your heart beat faster, your breath catch, your spirits lift, is worth a closer examination. But so too are feelings of anger, guilt, and torpor. When everything seems bleak and you have run out of wine, what is it that you want Jesus to do for you? And behind that immediate cry, what is it that you really want?

Focus for a time on the list of items you have high-lighted. Imagine Jesus looking at it with you and asking the question 'What do you want me to do for you?' If you had to sum up this list in one answer, what would that response be? Remember it is okay to answer with a question.

Often, when I ask people what they want, the answer is some kind of integration of life, including the sexual life, and faith. They seek a way of living out their beliefs about God and God's intention for the world that works. They sense that this way of life will be a journey towards their deepest, truest selves. Its destination being union with God the transcendent and immanent, the faraway mysterious one and the ever-so-near one. They are not deceived. We are told in Scripture that the Holy Spirit within us prays without ceasing. Surely this prayer of the Spirit must hold the answer to all our restless longings. If so it is important that we be hospitable to all our desires; some of them at least are prayers of the Spirit.

References

Smedes, Lewis, *Sex for Christians*. London, Triangle, 1993.

8

But If It Dies . . .

Intimacy requires that we let go.

I read recently in a newspaper of a Baptist minister who for many years had enjoyed a certain influence over his younger wife. He liked her to confine her activities to the home and she had done that. Then one day after 20 years of marriage she decided to take an Open University course. The husband put his foot down. He did not want her to study, meet people and generally widen her horizons. But his child bride was belatedly becoming a bolshy adolescent and the imminent demise of patriarchal domesticity stared him in the face. Friends watched horrified as the marriage disintegrated under the heavy burden of the husband's insistence that nothing change. The couple divorced. The woman started her studies.

There are times, many of them, in a good relationship when one partner or both must let go. Keeping things always the same, insisting that how it was is how it always must be, only results in a static relationship of superficiality where the inevitable cracks cut deep. When there is mutual love dependency is never the opposite of independence, intimacy is. There is a difference.

And intimacy invites us to let go, to dare even to die for the sake of life and love. The French call sexual orgasm *le petit mort*, the little death, and with good reason. The term recognizes that in intimacy, as in dying, a person is required to let go, surrendering themselves to an experience outwith their control. Those who cannot let go, perhaps because of some fear as yet unexplored or a wound unhealed, often find *le petit mort* elusive.

It was observing the seasons and the rhythms of life and death that taught Jesus that both are inextricably bound; that a single act of dying, of opening to the risk of nothingness can transform everything. He watched the farmers sowing seeds and found himself imagining a single grain of wheat acquiescing to the embrace of the cold, damp earth. Allowing itself to be changed by contact with this moist darkness; surrendering to gradual decomposition and patiently enduring a long period of silent isolation. At last the hidden life within can be held no longer in the frozen ground and bursts its way out, casting off the split seed-case and thrusting upwards in search of light and warmth. A new creation, so different from the seed, appears and itself contains thousands of seeds within.

As Passover approaches Jesus tells his disciples: 'Unless a wheat grain falls on the ground and dies it remains only a single grain; but if it dies, it yields a rich harvest' (John 12.24). It is not a lesson the companions want to hear and when Jesus turns his face towards Jerusalem, heading there in time for the Passover, they are afraid.

Peter, recently gifted with an insight into the person and mission of his Master and spokesman for the group, remonstrates with Jesus. I imagine him grabbing Jesus by the arm to hold him back:

'You can't possibly go to Jerusalem. (Not just now. It would be too dangerous.)

You might be arrested. (I might be arrested! The whole idea is ludicrous.)

They might even kill you. (They might kill me too!)

You cannot die. (I cannot die!)'

Peter is unable to grasp that at the heart of life lies the paschal mystery remembered and celebrated at each Passover, and now brought to completion in and through the body of Christ. And so poor Peter, having just confessed Jesus as 'The Christ, the Son of the Living God' (Matthew 16.16), almost immediately suffers a rebuke from Jesus: 'Get behind me Satan! You are an obstacle in my path, because the way you think is not God's way but man's' (Matthew 16.23). These are words that could be spoken to any of us. This way of thinking, that I cannot possibly die, is clearly not God's way of thinking at all. Otherwise, the voluntary death of the Son-made-man would have been inconceivable by the Trinity as a way of redeeming the world. But dying is a very modern taboo. It is the enemy of self-actualization and from our first breath to our last we resist it.

In the beginning, it may be inferred, our first cry, on being born, is the expression of our first experience of (painful) unfulfilled desire. We have emerged from the condition of having all our needs met without having to do anything; now we have to breathe and cry. We have no concept of ourselves or of anyone else; the universe and ourselves are one. The only distinctions we make are of total satisfaction – in which case we are either feeding or asleep – or of total pain – in which case the universe consists wholly of our screaming desire for food or the elimination of other bodily pain. (Klein, 1991)

Both experiences, the first of total satisfaction, the second of total pain, are unavoidable and quite natural. Through the one a baby is nurtured physically and emotionally and will develop a sense that the universe is kind. The other experience will teach her to insist on her own survival when danger threatens. Unfortunately this very useful and natural experience of existential fear, shared by the whole animal kingdom, invariably begets in humans a less healthy, indeed neurotic, fear of dying. It is the risk God takes in creation, one possible spin-off from the deep consciousness which differentiates ourselves from the rest of the animal kingdom.

We are not only aware of the movements and emotions within us but can use our will to determine the possibilities of our life. Little wonder then if, having fought so hard to survive the first helpless months of infancy, the id resolves never to die. Of course this resolve is unrealistic. All creatures must die. Indeed life holds for each of us many little deaths before the final one. These little deaths are appropriate and even necessary. The infant slips away and the child appears. The child disappears, as the boy Jesus disappeared for three days when he was 12 years old, and the adolescent comes noisily into the world. The adolescent gives way to the adult, and so on. There are other deaths. Some of our hopes and dreams do not survive, some relationships fade or are broken off, our mental and physical faculties slowly diminish over the years. Dying, though awesome, is natural. It is not in fact the enemy, but we think and act as though it is, resisting every dying with all our strength and will. In doing so we turn our back on the Kingdom and dwell in an alien land with fear as our god.

Many earnest and loving church folk offer superstitious worship to this idol in the hope that what they fear in life won't ever happen to them. They won't be made redundant, though someone in the department will. Their children won't experiment with drugs though the statistics show it more than likely. Their marriage will not break apart in spite of the lies and violence. Their tumour will not be malignant and it won't rain on their Sunday School picnic.

The gospel does not promise that bad things won't happen to good people who say their prayers. Instead it invites us to embrace the paschal mystery of life as grace. It offers as gift a deep awareness that, though the things we fear most in life are as likely as not to happen, nothing in our living or our dying can separate us from the love of God. 'Do not be afraid for I have redeemed you. I have called you by your name. You are mine' (Isaiah 43.1).

But a word of caution here. Though it is quite in order to ask God for a deeper awareness of the paschal mystery of life we must resist all heroic attempts to produce it like a rabbit from our Sunday-best hat. It is a grace. It is not a testimonial to the quality or depth of our faith. All we can do is ask God for it with as open a heart as we can manage. It is enough. God can and will do the rest.

With this grace we can go on to ask Jesus to show us the things that really must give way in our relationship to make room for something new. We all have attitudes, habits, assumptions, fears, expectations, pernicious and unhealthy games . . . that have had their season. This is true of our human partnership and our relationship with God. Recognizing them can be difficult in both cases so we need to be gentle with ourselves and ask for Jesus' help to grow into the truth about ourselves.

One useful place to look is in our frustrated desires. Whenever your honest response to the question 'What do I want?' seems impossible to have, then ask yourself 'Who says so?' Is it truly and appropriately impossible (perhaps because it would infringe on another person's rights) or is it merely impossible as things stand? If so what things stand in the way of your desire? Are these legitimate difficulties or are they perhaps an indication of some attitude, habit, etc. that needs to die?

'I want my partner to give me some space but I know that if I request this he will take it as confirmation that I am tiring of him.' The woman is in the habit of giving way to her partner's insecurities and he is in the habit of letting her. What might be possible once they both allow these habits to die, face their different fears and let God's grace address them?

'I want my wife to be less inhibited in our lovemaking but I am not sure if my desires are unreasonable.' The man is afraid and the source may be his oppressive religion, his internal parent or his wife's distaste at some of his requests. It would be useful for this couple to have a frank look at their attitudes to and expectations of sex, their sexual habits, the assumptions underlying these and any pernicious games of control that are secretly played by one to the disadvantage of both. Any of these might remain after such an examination but if some of them were allowed to die . . . what might become possible?

One man had learned in childhood not to ask his

parents for anything because the answer, for very practical reasons, was always 'No, we cannot afford it.' As a praying adult he discovered that he could not bring himself to ask God for anything either. He preferred to wait until providence threw an opportunity his way, then he would give thanks and happily enjoy the gift. But then one day God stopped playing this game of 'Catch', instead inviting the reluctant man to let go of his defensive approach and allow his passionate desires for life and service to be fully felt and acknowledged between them both. Dying to his old way of coping with life is taking some time, but there is little doubt that when this particular grain finally falls to the ground it will yield a most surprising harvest.

Now if the paschal mystery of life is a grace then Jesus must have experienced it as such. If it is a grace we find difficult to receive then we can be sure it was no easier for him than for us. When he spoke of grains of wheat he was trying to prepare his companions for some very difficult days ahead: his imminent arrest, trial and crucifixion. But I think he was also trying to come to terms with the probability of them himself. What he most feared was quite likely to happen, and happen soon. Was it really nothing to be afraid of?

The paschal mystery of Christ's life is the whole sequence of events from the moment Jesus enters Jerusalem on a donkey, to the moment when Mary Magdalene encounters the risen Christ in the garden on Easter morning. In one intense week Jesus experiences the welcome of the crowd shouting Hosannas, the betrayal of a friend, the celebration of three years of companionship with a tender farewell, doubt, fear, arrest, abuse, violence, abandonment and finally death itself. All this followed by the silence of the tomb, and then life bursting forth in a rush of passionate love and commitment.

Have you ever imagined the grace of love and trust that Jesus must have experienced in order to acquiesce to such a letting-go of life? His 'yes' in the Garden of Gethsemane was surely the most intimate moment of his passionate union with the Father and with the whole of creation. 'A man can have no greater love than to lay down his life for his friends' (John 15.13, 14). Likewise the Father letting the Son go to his death was the most intimate moment of God's passionate desire for us. 'God loved the world so much that he gave his only Son, so that everyone who believes in him may not be lost but may have eternal life' (John 3.16). Both the Father and the Son knew that just as the flower is entirely different from the seed, so the harvest of a man or woman's letting go is completely other, and infinitely more than can be imagined. They knew that if the Son dies then the harvest of this one death would be eternal.

A few years ago during a retreat I sought the grace to accompany Jesus in his Passion. There had been misunderstandings and difficulties as well as delights in our deepening relationship. But now I wanted to summon my courage and accompany Christ as his intimate friend, one to whom he could tell his darkest thoughts, his craziest longings, as he headed for the cross.

I wanted, as far as I was able, to be generous and open to the truth of his suffering. If you have ever accompanied a friend or relative in the final weeks before their death you will know this desire to be wholly available to another, to speak or remain silent, to help them put their affairs in order or plan next year's vacation. However they want to approach their illness and probable death, you will be there with them. So I prayed to stay with Jesus, if only by means of my imaginative prayer, as he endured the betrayal of friends, the loneliness of Gethsemane, the violent arrest, unjust trial, torture, hunger, humiliation and finally the awful suffering of a criminal's death on a cross.

I was struck by a passage from The Song of Songs where we find the world dealing harshly with the young girl and her passionate love. Tormented by the thought that her love is lost she agonizes:

> I looked for him but did not find him.
> I called him but he did not answer.
> The watchmen found me
> As they made their rounds in the city.
> They beat me, they bruised me,
> They took away my cloak,
> Those watchmen of the walls!
>
> Song of Songs 5.6–8 (NIV)

The girl runs frantically through the streets searching for her lover. She runs straight into the arms of the city watchmen on patrol. The watchmen assume she is a prostitute and take it upon themselves to punish her. The law demanded ritual exposure of a prostitute's nakedness but theirs is no lawful act. The men start to beat her up and as she struggles her clothes are torn from her body. She is battered and bruised, left half-naked to find her way home. No doubt the mocking laughter of the men was loud in the street.

It is dark night when these men take the law into their own hands and so severely mete out punishment to the frightened and friendless girl. Of course her own foolishness and impetuosity have led her into this grave danger. But then the watchmen too had a choice. They could have been kind, merciful, even supportive of her passionate quest. They chose to ridicule, turn a deaf ear to her distress and punish her for daring to flout the norms of behaviour.

In much the same way the world rejected Jesus and the revolutionary love he embodied. The truth is that for the girl, for Jesus, for any of us who pursue intimacy, the world and its hirelings will misunderstand and may even seek our ruin, concealing acts of violent hatred behind laws of economy and even of religion.

I tried to imagine what Jesus felt in the dark hours before his crucifixion and at the mercy of the world's hirelings:

He is lying on the floor. The soldiers gamble, drink, every so often dowsing him with water (not always fresh water) to keep him conscious of his agony.

I, the companion of Jesus, ask: 'What do you sense?'

I see blood, taste blood, smell blood and filth, hear blood rushing in my ears, and the soldiers' voices far off, then one coming closer. I feel everything shrinking in me. Then only pain.

'Do you know who you are?' (I feel the need to know that Jesus holds on to his mission.)

'I was a carpenter.' (He whispers, struggling to speak, struggling too, to remember.) 'I made things, from wood. Listened to children playing. My mother singing. The smell of bread baking. The white houses, salt on my lips. Laughed, and played with the wood beneath my fingers. And a dream. To make something beautiful. I thought I could . . .'

I feel tearful, plead with him to hear my words: 'You are the Christ! The Son of the Living God.'

Will it help? I am unsure. A long silence, then: 'Behold my Beloved Son . . .' (another dream from far away, of water and a dove).

This contemplation affected me in several ways. It opened my eyes to the vulnerability of Jesus during his Passion and to the surprising fact that my presence could comfort him. I was sorrowfully aware of my own neediness and fears in my selfish desire for a God who is invincible, whose mission to the world is guaranteed success.

Then in Jesus' words: 'I thought I could', my heart breaks for him, and gives birth to a resolve to help realize his dream of intimacy for the world, for me. I find myself wanting passionately to be the faithful companion of Christ, wherever I encounter him. To serve his cause wherever I find myself. And through it all to embrace the paschal mystery whenever I find it in my own experience.

I once suggested to a teacher that, at Easter time, he pray imaginatively with the paschal mystery of his own life. You may find this fruitful to do as he did. Beginning by looking for the Palm Sunday experiences of joy and celebration in his life he continued through the events of Holy Week allowing Jesus to identify for him his own paschal experiences. There were times when he felt betrayed or had let someone down, gracious farewells like that of Holy Thursday, times of lonely dread and times of cruel or unjust punishment. He identified times of entombment in darkness and confusion, but also Easter Sunday experiences; times of rebirth, or of dawning clarity, of wisdom, of strength. Times when he had emerged from a tomb into life, and this emerging had been unexpected and wildly energetic.

Not only did the teacher find the exercise personally fruitful, he took the idea into his primary class and asked the children to remember a Palm Sunday experience of their own. Some remembered huge family celebrations, a wedding or a picnic; others a prize-giving after a contest. The teacher invited the children to paint their memory. The next day, as the Easter break approached, the teacher asked them to remember a time of betrayal, and paint it. Children know about the paschal mystery of life, and these children were able to remember times in the playground or in the classroom or at home among siblings when they felt let down, even betrayed, by another. The teacher found that the exercises created a great deal of discussion and sharing among the children as well as a real identification with the suffering of Jesus. By now the success of the exercise had spread in the staff room and all the other teachers of different age groups were also using it as a fresh approach to the Easter story.

This identification even by small children with the Passion of Jesus is no accident. It is part of the reason why of such is the Kingdom of God. The paschal mystery with the cross at its centre is God's message of love. The Love of God which lies beyond any human knowledge or understanding finds meaning in Christ; intends Christ, creates through and for Christ, loves Christ alone, is inseparable from Christ, and perceives all things in the light of Christ. Christ is the Beloved Son, in whom God is well pleased. The mystery that a child knows before she knows anything else is this: I am part of Christ.

This brings us back to the question raised in chapter 5:

What went on when Jesus died on a cross? What has such a death to do with intimacy and with me? There are countless numbers of books written by theologians to explore the work of the cross. I have read very few of them. However, in contemplative prayer I have stood at the foot of the cross and, with a deep awareness of my being somehow involved in this drama, I have gazed on Christ's suffering and I have asked the question: 'What does this have to do with my life?' It is a question we might all usefully contemplate.

William Barclay, in his very readable book *Crucified and Crowned* (1961), looks to Paul's declaration at 1 Corinthians 15.3 to understand the atonement of the cross: 'Christ died for our sins in accordance with the scriptures.' Observing that the word 'for' has the meaning 'on behalf of' rather than 'because of' or 'in place of', Barclay says:

> The word atonement is really *at-one-ment*. We may, therefore, go on to say that the death of Jesus has done something which nothing else could ever do to make us *at one* with God. However we go on to interpret these basic statements – and the interpretations of them are many – we must begin with the two great kindred facts that Jesus died on behalf of the sins of men, and the effect of his death is to remove the estrangement between man and God and to make man and God *at one*.

Among the many interpretations of the basic statements are the following:

⋏ Jesus re-enacts, in his life, death and resurrection, the whole of humanity's history, but does it in the perfect obedience which was required of humanity, but which

we were unable to offer. The cross is about obedience
unto death.

⋏ Jesus was the *Christus Victor*; he finally and completely
defeated evil on the cross. The cross was a battle-
ground.

⋏ Jesus' death is the ransom paid to deliver humanity
from bondage. The cross is the place of transaction.

⋏ Jesus is the sacrifice that atones for our sin. The cross
is the altar I must approach but my offering is provided
by the Son.

⋏ Jesus on the cross satisfies God's requirement for punishment of sin. The cross restores God's honour.

⋏ Jesus is the substitution; he took the punishment that
was ours. The cross is my acquittal.

These are very brief sketches of only some atonement
theories. Wisely the Church has never chosen one as
holding the whole mystery. Consequently Christian folk
pick up these differing atonement theories through the
preached word, through hymns ancient and modern,
through Bible study and discussion and no doubt through
cliché. John Henry Newman wrote a hymn celebrating
Jesus, the one who recapitulates our history:

O loving wisdom of our God!
When all was sin and shame,
A second Adam to the fight
And to the rescue came.

O wisest love! That flesh and blood,
Which did in Adam fail,
Should strive afresh against the foe,
Should strive and should prevail;

While the well-known hymn by Cecil F. Alexander expresses the belief in Jesus as ransom:

> There was no other good enough
> To pay the price of sin;

And Frederick W. Faber draws our attention to the victory won on the cross:

> O love of God! O sin of man!
> In this dread act your strength is tried,
> And victory remains with love:
>
> *(The Church Hymnary, 1975)*

In one service of worship we might sing all of these atonement theories – a little confusing for anyone in the pews who actually listens to the words they are singing! For while many contribute a valuable insight, none of them says everything and one or two are actually unhelpful. Take a little time to ponder the atonement theories sketched above and see which ones are part of your own view of the cross, where these came from and how useful they have been to you.

On my retreat when I came with all these interpretations to contemplate in prayer the crucifixion of Jesus I experienced some difficulty imagining myself at the foot of the cross. Then I imagined that it was my elder son Jonathan who had been arrested, falsely accused, beaten up and tried in secret before being dragged out for public humiliation and brutal execution. Where would I be? How would I make sense of it all?

In my imagination he was on the cross to save my life. Simply because he loved me. Either he died without protest or we both would and though I was the mother, and willing enough to give my life to save his, that was never an option. I could only be there with him. I felt both intense pain and pride. And as I stood looking up my eyes pleaded with my son, 'Just look at me. Keep looking at my eyes. I am here and I know, I understand what you are doing and the love for me that has brought you to this.' I hoped that my own love and pride would pour out of my eyes and into his. Then I heard Christ whisper through Jonathan's eyes, 'Let me do this for you. Let me die.' It felt like a blow.

The Bible tells us that in God we live and move and have our being. Now I tried to grasp at something beyond my knowledge and experience. I hold *him* in being? And must I actually be the one to let him go? I sat with the enormity of this for several minutes trying to convince myself that I had misunderstood. But eventually I whispered back 'Jesus Christ, Son of God, go in peace.' It was a grace and a benediction.

In my prayer experience the cross was gift: the kind which is so hard to receive, so costly to the loved giver. I discovered that for me at least Christ died not to appease an angry God, to give due sacrifice to a remote God, to purchase my soul from the devil, or take humanity's place as a substitute in the punishment meted out by a just God. The truth was far more intimate.

Father, Son and Holy Spirit saw my personal difficulty; that I needed to be rescued not only from my neurotic resistance to intimacy and death but also from my distorted images of God and from guilt at my many failures to love. So God in Christ set about reconciling me to the reality of my life, my personality, my psychology. Christ saved my soul by letting go of his life in order to know and be known by me, his twin, in whom he lives and moves and has his being.

Imagine Christ on the cross if you can, and hear him ask you the question: 'Do you know what I have done to you?' What is your response? Mine is this: 'You have given your life to save my soul *from* mere existence and *for* intimacy both human and divine. Gazing at you on the cross I finally know with my whole soul – body, mind, spirit – that there is nothing standing between God and me; no break in our relationship, nothing of which to be afraid. It is done.'

But not quite done.

In the Song the girl returns home battered but still on fire with love. And too, with the death of Jesus and his battered, bruised body laid to rest, the last word on intimacy has not yet been spoken. For Love endures all things, believes all things, hopes all things. In the end Love conquers all. The last word is resurrection. The Christian faith asserts that Jesus, the one crucified, was raised to life by God. If Christ is indeed risen then it is possible for me to experience a deep sense of Christ's joy and consolation at his resurrection. Such an experience, of course, would be pure grace. When we look to Scripture for passages to contemplate the resurrection it is the Song of Songs that is our most evocative source. One such passage begins with those verses we contemplated earlier where the lover is likened to a gazelle leaping over the mountain. The passage goes on:

> Behold, standing by our wall,
> Peeping in at the window,
> Peering in through the lattice.
> He responded my lover, and said to me,
> 'Arise my darling,
> My beautiful one, and come.'
> For behold, the winter has passed,

The rain has passed, has gone.
The blossoms have appeared in the land;
The time of singing has drawn near,
And the voice of the turtle-dove is heard in our land.
The fig tree has sprouted her early fruits
And the vines in blossom have yielded their scent.
'Arise, come my love,
My beautiful one, and come.'

(Song of Songs 2.9–13)

Since we are in Christ and Christ in us intimacy requires of us all a little dying. To know Christ is to know and understand that, thanks to Christ's sacrifice of himself, the pain of each death is nothing in comparison to the joy of each resurrection. To be known by Christ is to accept the paschal mystery of life. Can you see where this has been true in your life, faith and relationship?

For each moment of dying followed by new birth try to imagine Christ leaping from the tomb and dancing across the hills to stand outside your window in delighted mirth. After winter comes the spring. After death comes life eternal. After the tomb comes the dance of passionate intimacy. Arise, come. You are the beautiful one, the beloved. Come.

References

Barclay, William, *Crucified and Crowned*. London, SCM Press, 1961.

The Church Hymnary. 3rd edn. London, Oxford University Press, 1975.

Gledhill, Tom, *The Message of The Song of Songs*. Leicester, IVP, 1994.

Klein, Mavis, *Okay Parenting – A Psychological Handbook for Parents*. London, Piatkus Books, 1991.

9

Do You Love Me?

Intimacy leads to intimacy.

In the musical 'Fiddler on the Roof', the main character is a Jewish husband and father married by arrangement 25 years ago and now watching bemused as his three elder daughters break from tradition. Each one of them insists on marrying the man of their own choice, the one with whom they have fallen in love.

Afraid for his daughters but also filled with self-doubt, the man asks his wife in song: 'Do you love me?' She responds incredulously: 'Do I *love* you?' and goes on to list all the things she has done on a daily basis for him over the past 25 years. Still the man insists on the question: 'Yes, but do you *love* me?' He has a point.

There is a story at the end of John's Gospel that contains rich insight into the grace needed for any marriage that hopes not only to endure but to triumph over the adversities of life. It is the resurrection appearance of Christ to Peter and the disciples on the shore of the Sea of Tiberias.

It was light by now and there stood Jesus on the shore, though the disciples did not realize that it was Jesus.

Jesus called out, 'Have you caught anything, friends?' And when they answered, 'No', he said, 'Throw the net out to starboard and you'll find something'. So they dropped the net, and there were so many fish that they could not haul it in. The disciple Jesus loved said to Peter, 'It is the Lord'. At these words 'It is the Lord', Simon Peter, who had practically nothing on, wrapped his cloak round him and jumped into the water. The other disciples came on in the boat, towing the net and the fish; they were only about a hundred yards from land. (John 21.4–8)

The companions breakfasted on the cooked fish. When everyone had eaten and the excited conversations had quieted a little Jesus drew Peter apart and as they strolled together along the shore turned to face him:

'Simon son of John, do you love me more than these others do?' He answered, 'Yes Lord, you know I love you.' Jesus said to him, 'Feed my lambs.' A second time he said to him, 'Simon son of John, do you love me?' He replied, 'Yes, Lord, you know I love you.' Jesus said to him, 'Look after my sheep.' Then he said to him a third time, 'Simon son of John, do you love me?' Peter was upset that he asked him the third time, 'Do you love me?' and said, 'Lord, you know everything; you know I love you.' Jesus said to him, 'Feed my sheep.' (John 21.15–17)

'Do you love me?' he asks three times. We cannot know where the emphasis was placed each time Jesus asked the question but we do know that the Gospel-writer used two of the four different Greek words for the word 'love'.

144

Do You Love Me?

Twice the Gospel has Jesus use the word *agape* for love. Each time Peter responds with *philia*, which is more like saying, in the manner of the Jewish wife, 'Yes, Lord, you know I care for you.' Poor Peter. Still raw from his own triple denial of this friendship he is unsure what depth of feeling he has or has the right to have for his Lord.

We know just how he feels. Betrayal is inevitable whenever people seek intimacy together. In countless ways, significant and trivial, we betray our closest, most intimate companions and are betrayed by them. The effect can be devastating to intimacy and can shatter our own self-trust. Yet, inevitable as it is, very few of us are not taken by surprise each time betrayal occurs. We expect ourselves or this other to remain constant, to be perfectly wise and sensitive, to know at every turn of events the appropriate action to take. Not so Jesus.

Recall how the disciples in the upper room questioned among themselves who among them could possibly betray his friendship. Jesus knew the answer. All of them would at some time, in various ways. And in particular Judas and Peter, two of his most intimate companions, would betray him very soon.

But here on the beach, with the morning sun climbing into the sky throwing the memory of cross and tomb into silhouette in their minds, mercy is the grace on offer. Because Love rather than sufferance had conquered all, passionate mercy rather than dutiful forgiveness would now reclaim Peter from his despair. And besides, *philia* is just not what Jesus has in mind for the rock on which to build a church. He has a point.

There is a difference between caring deeply for someone and loving them. I care deeply for my dog and for his welfare, but do I love a dog? I enjoy his company, feed, exercise, take him to the vet and arrange decent accommodation in kennels when I go on holiday. Is that love? I hope not.

I hope love is more than all the care and practical concern I show for my partner. I hope it is something beyond the routine and compromise of shared space and resources. I want it to be a mystical union of two souls; a spiritual as well as an emotional and physical reality. When I ask my husband if he loves me I want to know if he feels united to me body, mind, soul so that he no longer knows where he ends and I begin.

The answer is likely to be 'Sometimes'. A good enough response. It reflects our experience together of ecstasy: that momentary melting of the natural boundaries between two individuals. And who knows? – intimacy may lead to intimacy for there is always more grace. Then whenever life on this earth is over we will be as indivisible as we are intimate. Not, I think, in the way that Siamese twins are indivisible but rather as are the flame and light of a candle.

This at least seems to be how the risen Christ felt about things as he changed tack with Peter. The third time Jesus asks Peter 'Do you love me?' he himself uses *philia*. The effect is dramatic. Peter, hearing his own choice of word reflected back to him, is so distressed by its inadequacy and lack of intimacy that he brokenly confesses his true depth of feeling: 'Lord, you know everything; you know I love (*agape*) you.'

Once more Peter is gifted with an insight that surely comes straight from the Father's heart. When a soul is fully known and understood mercy is inevitable. And as

Do You Love Me?

Portia tells Shylock:

> The quality of mercy is not strain'd –
> It droppeth as the gentle rain from heaven
> Upon the place beneath: it is twice bless'd,
> It blesseth him that gives, and him that takes:
> 'Tis mightiest in the mightiest: it becomes
> The throned monarch better than his crown;
> His sceptre shows the force of temporal power,
> The attribute to awe and majesty,
> Wherein doth sit the dread and fear of kings;
> But mercy is above this sceptred sway,
> It is enthroned in the heart of kings,
> It is an attribute of God himself,
> And earthly power doth then show likest God's
> When mercy seasons justice. Therefore, Jew,
> Though justice be thy plea, consider this:
> That, in the course of justice, none of us
> Should see salvation. We do pray for mercy;
> And that same prayer doth teach us all to render
> The deeds of mercy. . .

> (*The Merchant of Venice*, Act IV, scene 1)

Mercy like this, stemming from profound understanding and so unlike sufferance, is a grace. A jewel of a grace and not something we can strain towards by our own effort. But it is a grace we all have need of many times in the routine of life and one we should all seek to render to others. With the grace of mercy all things are possible.

On the cross Jesus experienced an intimate knowledge of every soul that was, is or ever will be born. Jesus knows Peter better than Peter knows or understands himself.

147

Now finally Peter understands this and realizes that his awful denial is completely understood in all its grim detail and just as completely forgiven.

In our relationship with partner or with God, however deep the grace of intimacy we enjoy, we cannot know everything about this other. Fortunately, and because of the cross, a deep awareness of one simple truth can fill the gap of our knowledge. It is recorded for us in the Song of Songs: 'My beloved is mine and I am his' (2.16). What confidence there is in this declaration! The young lovers are forever intimately united not because they are always together or because they will never make a mistake in their relationship but because they are resolved to be so. My beloved is mine and I am his. It's a done deal.

The same commitment is made in the marriage ceremony. Before God we declare our resolve: My beloved is mine and I am my beloved's. This vow of belonging is not only a declaration of intimacy but a commitment to intimacy. Friends and family witness both. They in turn pledge themselves to succour this relationship whenever difficulties arise for the couple. In our relationship with Christ we make this same resolve, and Christ makes it to us, each time we receive the Sacrament. My beloved Church is mine and I am my beloved's. The resolve helps fill the gap of knowledge by helping each individual discern the merciful response in any situation. In times of betrayal, devastating or irritating, of God or our partner the power of mercy facilitated by this simple truth can reclaim us and restore our relationship.

Take some time to imagine yourself into this beach scene. Hear Jesus ask: 'Do you love me?' Do not rush to answer. Honour the questioner by allowing the question time to make its impact on you. The Lord of all life wants to know how *you* feel about him. He is seeking your intimate friendship, loyalty, company. Become aware of guilt feelings surrounding any aspect of your life that prevent your wholehearted confession of love. Become aware too that Jesus has plumbed the depths of your being and declares, 'My beloved is mine and I am his'. Jesus requests that you have mercy on yourself. Ponder what form this mercy for self might take. Ask for the grace of a deep awareness that for you Jesus is the beloved and that you indeed are beloved by him.

Discerning mercy is the work-a-day grace vital to a life that is complex and problematic from the first breath to the last. Without it relationship is difficult, gratitude is rare, and intimacy impossible. Most breakdowns of marriages and relationships occur in the first ten years. It is as though the discoveries coming thick and fast of a partner's imperfections become intolerable over the course of that first decade. We feel betrayed. And accuse the other, audibly or silently, of not being the person we married (or intended to marry). Without the grace of mercy the accusation is likely to stick.

Betrayal is also common enough in marriages of any duration when they run out of wine. Mercifully, few relationships end with one partner betraying the other to his/her death as Judas did. But too many have felt the death blow of a partner exchanging the exclusivity of the relationship for the excitement or distraction of a clandestine affair. Alternatively one partner in an effort to save his/her happiness may do as Peter did. In words or actions the declaration is made: 'I don't know you any more' or 'I never really knew you' or 'You are nothing to me'. All too often we witness the bitter fruits of this denial in the divorce-courts. We watch horrified as friends of ours who have shared life, love, children, now deny even the most basic duty of courtesy to one another.

Judas and Peter betrayed their friend. Despair overtook Judas before mercy could intervene. But for Peter, on the shore that morning, the story is quite different. He allows the risen Christ to reclaim him from his despair. How often in our relationships do we choose, in our independence and pride, to be more Judas than Peter. Yet the grace of mercy is available to us all. One partner can be the risen Christ reclaiming the other from despair. The message of the cross is forgiveness. Life beyond the most painful death, hope beyond the deepest of betrayals, mercy gently dropping from heaven.

We read in the story how Peter confesses his love (still an imperfect, inconstant thing) and accepts forgiveness. Then Jesus draws Peter to him and whispers close to his ear the manner of death that Peter could expect and then says: 'Follow me' (John 21.19). Here is a new invitation, different to 'Come and see'. With it the risen Christ acknowledges Peter as intimate companion; one who has seen and understood. It is an invitation to further intimacy and one given to all of us on a daily basis. Moreover, it is an invitation to dance rather than plod behind Christ. The risen Christ is full of joy and dances through this world. Accepting his invitation means joining with the dancing Trinity both individually and as a couple.

There is no need to cling to each other as we whirl across the floor. Since my beloved is mine and I am my beloved's the lightest of touch will keep us together as we synchronize our moves to the music of creation. We are increasingly skilled partners and our timing, motion and steps display a unity that is as good to watch as it is to enjoy. As a dancing duo we will become playful and confident, able to articulate our desires and willing to be in turns seduced and seducer. Between us we will develop skills of tact, patience, humour and honesty along with perseverance that comes in useful whenever things go pear-shaped. And our resolve – 'I am my beloved's and my beloved is mine' – continues to be a touchstone of discernment as intimacy leads to intimacy.

Experience taught Ignatius that not every thought, inspiration, inclination, desire or mood that rose in him, even during a time of concentrated prayer, came from God. Some of it came from the cheese he ate for supper. Lots of it arose from his own personality and upbringing. A little came from God, but some came from a resistance to God. All of this Ignatius understood to be quite usual and part of the human condition. Even at the very best of times in our life of intimacy with God or with our partner we too can expect to experience a bewildering variety of thoughts, moods, insights and inclinations. Contemplating these in relation to our resolve will help us identify which are conducive to intimacy and which are not.

Ignatius was sure that discernment was possible in a relationship when each person is committed to the other exclusively. He formed some guidelines to help a person in this kind of relationship with God discern among the choices in life which would lead to greater unity with God, the Beloved. Guidelines that can also be useful in a human partnership.

In either case the guiding principle is simple: I want only what is good for the relationship we share. So while

I work with my diverse desires I have in mind my resolve
that I am my beloved's and he is mine. Any desire that
works against this cannot be a desire worth pursuing.
Discernment is a grace of skill and it requires practice if I
am to distinguish between desires that look as though
they have intimacy as their destiny and those that actually
do. How many men (and even whole societies) have
justified adultery by telling themselves that it actually
enhances a marriage and so benefits both partners without doing any harm (since it is kept hidden)?

Few of us may consider ourselves capable of this
absurdity. We are capable however of overlooking the
damage done to intimacy by the society-sanctioned drive
for success prevalent in the developed world. We enjoy
the status, wealth, satisfaction to both partners it brings,
choosing to ignore even the most immediate spin-offs:
misery, alienation from children and ultimately the subtle
destruction of intimacy. If I am my beloved's and he/she is
mine my career, my vaulting ambition, my pride must
surely take a place lower down in my priorities than the
quality and durability of this vocation we share.

What might be possible if the whole population of this
earth refused to sanction the worship of that triple deity
wealth, power and honour and together withheld their
sacrifice of inappropriate blood, sweat and tears to this
idol for even one day? What if we took a stand together
and declared that the end does not in fact justify the
means? Nothing less than a new order might be ushered
in as suddenly as the collapse of that other man-made
structure – the Berlin Wall – occurred. Nothing less than
a new order is what Christ is about. Intimacy leads to
intimacy and we, like Peter, are invited to follow where

the dance of intimacy leads. Christ's transformation of us, our relationship, our world, requires our co-operation.

It is time to imagine yourself hearing this invitation and see yourself falling into step with Christ as Peter did on the shore of Lake Tiberias. You are a companion of Christ, trusted by him, beloved of him, wanted by him. Imagine what a good friend might feel watching you walk or dance with Christ. Try to frame the prayer that friend might earnestly make for you now.

Then consider your partner in a similar scene. This person too is a companion of Christ; trusted by him, beloved by him, wanted by him. Imagine your partner falling into step with Christ and talking intimately and freely with him, as they walk into the distance. Let them go and whisper a prayer for your partner.

Then one final time imagine the scene. This time imagine that Christ watches with a prayer on his lips as both of you dance across the sands and into the future. Catch the whisper of his prayer on the breeze. What is the grace Christ wants for you both now? Surely that intimacy will lead to intimacy until it ignites finally into a transforming flame of passion. All for the greater glory of God. Amen.

References

Shakespeare, William, *The Merchant of Venice*. Cambridge, Cambridge University Press, 1992.